Thom Gunn

in conversation with

James Campbell

Thom Gunn

in conversation with

James Campbell

Between The Lines

First published in 2000 by

BTL
Between The Lines

9 Woodstock Road
London N4 3ET
UK

Tel: +44 (0)20 7272 8719
Fax: +44 (0)20 8374 5736

E-mail: betweenthelines@lineone.net
Website: http://www.interviews-with-poets.com

© Questions: James Campbell
© Answers: Thom Gunn
© 'Clean Clothes: a soldier's song': Thom Gunn
© Photograph of Thom Gunn: Ander Gunn

The right of James Campbell to be identified as the author of this work
has been asserted by him in accordance with
the Copyright, Designs and Patents Act of 1988

All rights reserved

A CIP catalogue record for this book
is available from the British Library

ISBN 1 903291 00 3

Jacket design and artwork: Philip Hoy

Printed and bound by
Biddles Ltd
Unit 26
Rollesby Road
Hardwick Industrial Estate
King's Lynn
Norfolk PE30 4LS
UK

Between The Lines

EDITORIAL BOARD

PETER DALE — IAN HAMILTON — PHILIP HOY — J.D. MCCLATCHY

BTL publishes more than usually wide-ranging and more than usually deep-going interviews with some of today's most accomplished poets.

Some would deny that any useful purpose is served by putting to a writer questions which are not answered by that writer's books. For them, what Yeats called 'the bundle of accident and incoherence that sits down to breakfast' is best left alone, not asked to interrupt its cornflakes, or to set aside its morning paper, while someone with a tape recorder inquires about its life, habits and attitudes.

If we do not share this view, it is not because we endorse Sainte-Beuve's dictum, *tel arbre, tel fruit* — as the tree, so the fruit — but because we understand what Geoffrey Braithwaite was getting at when the author of *Flaubert's Parrot* had him say:

> 'But if you love a writer, if you depend upon the drip-feed of his intelligence, if you want to pursue him and find him — despite edicts to the contrary — then it's impossible to know too much.'

Volumes 1-5, featuring W.D. Snodgrass, Michael Hamburger, Anthony Thwaite, Anthony Hecht, and Donald Hall, respectively, are already available; others now being prepared will feature Richard Wilbur, Seamus Heaney, Paul Muldoon, Donald Justice and Hans Magnus Enzensberger. (Further details are given overleaf.)

As well as the interview, each volume will contain a sketch of the poet's life and career, a comprehensive bibliography, archival information, and a representative selection of quotations from the poet's critics and reviewers. It is hoped that the results will be of interest to the lay reader and specialist alike.

— Other volumes from BTL —

W.D. Snodgrass
in conversation with Philip Hoy
ISBN 0-9532841-0-7

Michael Hamburger
in conversation with Peter Dale
ISBN 0-9532841-1-5

Anthony Thwaite
in conversation with Peter Dale and Ian Hamilton
ISBN 0-9532841-2-3

Anthony Hecht
in conversation with Philip Hoy
ISBN 0-9532841-3-1

Donald Hall
in conversation with Ian Hamilton
ISBN 0-9532841-4-X

— Forthcoming —

Richard Wilbur
in conversation with Peter Dale
ISBN 0-9532841-5-8

Seamus Heaney
in conversation with Karl Miller
ISBN 0-9532841-7-4

Paul Muldoon
in conversation with Lavinia Greenlaw
ISBN 0-9532841-8-2

Donald Justice
in conversation with Philip Hoy
ISBN 0-9532841-9-0

Hans Magnus Enzensberger
in conversation with Michael Hulse and John Kinsella
ISBN 0-9532841-6-6

CONTENTS

Acknowledgements   9

A Portrait of Thom Gunn   10

A Note on Thom Gunn   11

A Note on James Campbell   13

The Conversation   15

'Clean Clothes: a soldier's song', by Thom Gunn   57

Bibliography   59

The Critics   103

Acknowledgements

A shorter version of this interview was originally broadcast on BBC Radio 3's *Postscript*, under the title, 'Between Moving Air and Moving Ocean'. It is reproduced here by kind permission of the BBC. The series of programmes was produced by Sara Davies. Also taking part, in a supplementary programme, were Wendy Lesser, Karl Miller, Hugo Williams and Clive Wilmer.

The editors would like to thank Thom Gunn for permission to use his uncollected poem, 'Clean Clothes: a soldier's song', which appears on page 57.

They would also like to thank Ander Gunn for permission to use the photograph of his brother which appears overleaf.

Last, but by no means least, the editors would like to thank Jack W.C. Hagstrom, George Bixby and Joshua Odell, without whose painstaking research (published and unpublished) the bibliography printed on pages 59-102 would not have been possible.

Thom Gunn

photograph courtesy of
Ander Gunn

©

A Note on Thom Gunn

Thom Gunn was born in Gravesend, Kent, in August 1929, the elder son of Herbert and Ann Charlotte Gunn (née Thomson). His father was a successful journalist who, after many years spent working on provincial newspapers, moved to London, where he became editor, first of the *Evening Standard,* and then, somewhat later, of the *Daily Sketch*. Gunn's mother had also been a journalist, but gave up her career with the births of Thom and his younger brother, Ander.

Gunn was only eight years old when the family moved to London, settling in Hampstead. He remembers the time and the place with great affection, and speaks of his boyhood as a very happy one. Just two years after the move, however, his parents were divorced. And four years after *that,* when Gunn was still in his mid-teens, his mother committed suicide. Asked about these events, and their effect on him, Gunn's inclination has been to ask whether all adolescences aren't unhappy, and to leave it at that.

Gunn's love of reading seems to have been inspired by his mother, whose books filled the house. By the time of her death, he was immersed in the writings of Marlowe, Keats, Milton and Tennyson – to mention only the poets – and was unquestioningly committed to the idea 'of books as not just a commentary on life but as a part of its continuing activity.'

After leaving school, Gunn did two years of National Service, and then went up to Cambridge. He was twenty-one, and by his own account – and notwithstanding his precocity as a reader – 'strangely immature'. But, surrounded by lively and challenging contemporaries – Karl Miller, John Coleman, John Mander, Tony White, and Mark Boxer, amongst them – Gunn came of age, as can be seen from the poems he began to write at this time, poems which were to make up his first book.

Fighting Terms appeared in 1954, the year after Gunn's graduation, to considerable acclaim. 'This is one of the few volumes of postwar verse that all serious readers of poetry need to possess and to study,' wrote the critic, John Press, and few dissented. As Timothy Steele put it more recently: 'Impressive for their concentration, their vigour, and their effective fusion of traditional metre with contemporary idiom, these poems established [Gunn] as one of the most arresting voices of his generation.'

While an undergraduate, Gunn met Mike Kitay, an American. After leaving Cambridge, he followed Kitay to the United States, something made possible by the award of a creative writing fellowship at Stanford University, where he became a student of the poet and critic, Yvor Winters. Except for the occasional visit, and one year-long sojourn in the mid-'60s, Gunn was never to return to England. He had decided to make America his home, and in 1960 settled in San Francisco, the city where he has lived ever since.

Eight major collections have appeared since *Fighting Terms* – *The Sense of Movement* (1957), *My Sad Captains* (1961), *Touch* (1967), *Moly* (1971), *Jack Straw's Castle* (1976), *The Passages of Joy* (1982), *The Man with Night Sweats* (1992), and, most recently, *Boss Cupid* (2000). Not all of them have been as enthusiastically received as that first book, however. Especially during the '70s and '80s, when he started to write out of his experiences as a user of soft and hard drugs, and to write more openly of his life as a homosexual, there were a number of critics who felt that he was squandering his talent, indulging in what one called 'hippy silliness', or abandoning himself to what another called 'vacant counter-cultural slovenliness'.

With publication of *The Man with Night Sweats,* a collection which memorialized friends and acquaintances who had fallen victim to AIDS, those who had come to think of Gunn as a poet who had failed to live up to his early promise were obliged to reconsider. As Neil Powell, a long-standing but not uncritical admirer, put it: 'In [the final section of the book] Gunn restores poetry to a centrality it has often seemed close to losing, by dealing in the context of a specific human catastrophe with the great themes of life and death, coherently, intelligently, memorably. One could hardly ask for more.'

Gunn has received a large number of awards and prizes for his work, amongst them the Levinson Prize (1955), the Somerset Maugham Award (1959), an Arts Council of Great Britain Award (1959), an American Institute of Arts and Letters Grant (1964), an American Academy Grant (1964), a Rockefeller Award (1966), a Guggenheim Fellowship (1971), the W.H. Smith Award (1980), the PEN (Los Angeles) Prize for Poetry (1983), the Sara Teasdale Prize (1988), the Los Angeles Times Kirsch Award (1988), the Lila Wallace/Reader's Digest Writer's Award (1990), the Forward Prize (1992), the Lenore Marshall Prize (1993), and a MacArthur Fellowship (1993).

A Note on James Campbell

James Campbell was born in Glasgow and educated at Edinburgh University. Between 1978 and 1982, he was the editor of the *New Edinburgh Review*. He is the author of several books of non-fiction, including *Talking at the Gates: A Life of James Baldwin* (1991); *Paris Interzone: Richard Wright, Lolita, Boris Vian and Others on the Left Bank* (1994); and *This Is the Beat Generation* (1999). In addition, he has edited the *Picador Book of Blues and Jazz*, and written a play, *The Midnight Hour*, which has been performed in the United States and France. He lives in London, where he works for the *Times Literary Supplement*.

The Conversation

The following interview took place in January 1999. It was conducted over three days, with Gunn and his interviewer seated at the long living-room table in the poet's house in the Haight-Ashbury district of San Francisco. Also in attendance was Sara Davies, the BBC producer there to record the proceedings for Radio 3.
  The programmes, which were broadcast on four consecutive evenings in May 1999, presented an abridged version of the interview, their duration necessitating cuts. We have restored almost all of the cut material, while making some small adjustments to the order of presentation.

Do you remember any of your earliest poems, the ones you wrote when you were still a child?

I can read you something I wrote when I was about eleven. It was called 'A Thousand Cheers for Authors', and the second half went like this:

> In Mr Bumpus's bookshop,
> Oh there is my delight,
> Of books he has a monster crop,
> They are a lovely sight.
> I hope that authors never stop
> For reading gives the wisdom light.
> A thousand cheers for authors!
>
> I love to think of books of old
> The great Greeks wrote so long ago,
> Chaucer the first English stories told,
> Sweet Shakespeare came, and stout Defoe,
> With Jonathan Swift and Bunyan bold,
> Till Dumas – he's the best I know –
> A thousand cheers for authors!

The poem came out in a school magazine, otherwise it would be completely forgotten.

You wrote that when you were a schoolboy at University College in Hampstead, north London.

Yes.

Where was Bumpus's Bookshop?

I think it was on Oxford Street. It was quite a famous bookshop. I have an edition of *Paradise Lost* that was published by Bumpus at, I think, the same address, in 1811, or thereabouts.

Was it your teachers who recommended you to go there?

No, it was just known to be a good bookshop, and I used to get my copies of E. Nesbit and, later, Dumas, from there.

Did you have good teachers at the University College School?

My first teacher, at the junior branch – which is where I wrote that poem – was a certain Miss Polameni. She was wonderful, a very good English and History teacher. But by the time I got to the senior school, the war was on, and many of the teachers were past normal retirement age. The English teacher, particularly. I won't name him, though I'm sure he's dead by now.

Your father was a journalist. Was it he who gave you your introduction to books?

No, he didn't read books very much. My mother used to say he never read any books except detective stories and books about journalism. No, *she* was the great reader.

Was she a sophisticated woman?

Yes, she told me she'd read Gibbon's *Decline and Fall* when she was pregnant with me – which may say something about me, though I don't know what – and she'd recommend Jane Austen and things like that when she thought I was old enough to start reading them. I gobbled them up.

And you wrote a novel at her request, when you were twelve. You must have been a very devoted son.

I think I was eleven. It was during the Blitz, and I'd just got sent to a boarding school, Bedales, and I said, 'What shall I give you for your birthday?' and she said, 'Why don't you write me a novel?' Every day there was a siesta after lunch, and I'd get bored – I never felt like napping – so I'd write a chapter of this so-called novel. Actually, if it were printed, it would be about ten pages long, the whole thing. But there were about fifty chapters, short ones. It was called *The Flirt*.

When did you first know that you were willing to dedicate your life to poetry? Was it when you were an adolescent, or did it come later?

It was much later. I was always attracted by the idea of writing, since, as you can tell from that early poem, I liked books a lot. I was a bookish boy. I tried writing short stories, and I tried writing novels, and I tried writing plays. None of these ever got finished, except the short stories, I guess. I tried writing poetry as well – it was all *dreadful* stuff – but eventually, round the age of twenty or so, I realized I was more enthusiastic about poetry than the other forms, so that was what I wrote.

Did you have a happy childhood altogether?

I had an extraordinarily happy childhood, yes. Until my mother's death, but that wasn't till I was about fifteen.

So it must have been a childhood which was quite starkly divided between happiness and unhappiness? Before and after your mother died, I mean.

Yes, but you know I was hardly a child any longer: I was an adolescent by then. Everybody has an unhappy adolescence, don't they? All those chemical changes going on inside your body are so distressing and unexpected.

What happened after your mother's death?

I divided my time – or my time was divided – between continuing to go to the school in Hampstead while living with a family who'd been friends of my mother's, and spending the weekends and vacations down in Snodland in Kent with two of my aunts.

What was the family like that took you in?

The people who took me in were extraordinarily kind. This hadn't been what they'd got planned for their lives. Suddenly to have this great gawky boy, with all the awkwardness of adolescence, thrust upon them, must have been very difficult for them. But of course you don't realize that at the time. You think that adults were made to look after you, that their main purpose in life was to care for people your age.

I was wondering if the poem 'Autobiography', which is in Jack Straw's Castle, *is about this period in your life. And the lines, in particular, 'life seemed all / loss, and what was more / I'd lost whatever it was / before I'd even had it.' Are you experiencing real loss here, or is it ironically self-pitying?*

I think I'm making a joke. In fact, I know I'm making a joke. It's this kind of desolate feeling you have as an adolescent that you're never going to be any good as an adult and nothing's going to come out right. Everybody has that.

You've said 'almost everything that figures importantly in my life finds its way sooner or later into poetry.' But it takes longer to write about some things than others, doesn't it? Why did it take you so long to feel you could write about your father?

Well, you have to find a way of doing these things. Where *did* I write about my father? I'm not sure I did. Oh, maybe I did ...

The first poem in Moly.

I suppose that can be considered to be about my father, yes. — Well, as I say, you have to find a way of doing these things. The first poem I wrote about the AIDS epidemic was about a very close friend of mine who died — he was the first of my friends to die from this — and I started writing that poem the day after his death. I was amazed that I knew how to do it so soon. Other things you may wait twenty years to write. But all writers have this experience. At first you don't know how to put things together, and then, after a time, you find they have all come together, magically, and at last you can write about them.

Your new book, Boss Cupid, *contains some poems about your mother. Is this the first time you've written about her?*

There are a couple of poems about my mother in the new book. One's a very short little poem called 'My Mother's Pride'. I think it's organized in the same way as Pound's Canto XIII, which is a slightly random collection of sayings by Confucius. I brought her sayings together in the same kind of way: 'Never pay attention to the opinions of strangers,' 'Only conceited children are shy' ... The second poem about my mother is called 'The Gas Poker'. She killed herself, and my brother and I found her body, which was not her fault because she'd barred the doors, as you'll see in the poem. Obviously this was quite a traumatic experience; it would be in anybody's life. I wasn't able to write about it till just a few years ago. Finally I found the way to do it was really obvious: to withdraw the first-person, and to write about it in the third-person. Then it came easy, because it was no longer about myself. I don't like dramatizing myself. I don't want to be Sylvia Plath. The last person I want to be! I was trying in this poem to objectify the situation:

> Forty-eight years ago
> – Can it be forty-eight
> Since then? – they forced the door
> Which she had barricaded
> With a full bureau's weight
> Lest anyone find, as they did,
> What she had blocked it for.

I think I probably got a bit of help from Thomas Hardy writing that poem, the emphasis on the rather awkward, forced, rhymes: *barricaded / they did,* and so on.

Was it in your late teens that you discovered your homosexuality?

Well, it is a very difficult thing for anybody to know when they really discovered their 'sexual orientation', as we politely call it nowadays. I don't know when I discovered it. I was extraordinarily dishonest with myself in my late teens: all my sexual fantasies were about men, but I assumed I was straight. I think it was partly because homosexuality was such a forbidden subject in those days. My parents didn't seem to have any queer friends. The only adult homosexuals I knew about seemed to be old men waiting patiently in urinals, hour after hour, and I didn't want to be one of them. I didn't want to be effeminate either; I didn't think that was me. I would love to have met some sporty young man who seduced me, but no, that wasn't to happen.

How long was it before it happened?

It was at Cambridge.

Did you have the usual fumblings with girls, first of all?

Yes, pretty clumsy. As clumsy as if I'd been straight.

Before you went up to Cambridge, you did your National Service. Did anything good come out of that? Do you think back on it as a happy experience?

No, I don't think of it as a happy experience. I think of it as an experience of prolonged boredom. But I did find out something about my limits. I was a spoilt little middle-class boy, and it was good for me in basic training to have to sleep between blankets. It was also good for me to have to accept that ignorant people were in power over me and to have to deal with that as intelligently as I could. I learned a lot of negative things that it was about time I learned. I don't regret anything that's happened to me, and I don't regret National Service, but it did contain a lot of wasted time, boredom, drudgery.

Did you have political views at that time?

Oh yes, we were all left-wing in my generation. When I was at school, at the time of the 1945 landslide, most of us were Labour, and I can remember hearing the older boys speculating about who had written a book that came out from Gollancz under the pseudonym of *Cato*. *I* knew who it was by. I knew it was by Michael Foot, because my father and my stepfather were both journalists, and they'd mentioned it in conversation. When I went to Cambridge, several years later, in 1950, we were still all socialists then. Even people like Norman Podhoretz and Hugh Thomas – who were both at Cambridge when I was there – were left-wing at that time. I'm *still* a socialist, unlike them.

A lot of people drift in and out of university without really having noticed that it happened. Was that the case with you?

No, it was tremendously important to me. It was an escape into my life. It was then that I started to spell my first name with 'h'. It seemed to me to be nothing more than a delightful affectation when I came to Cambridge, but I can now see that this was an attempt to become a new person; it was my announcement that I was going to be somebody new. When I arrived, I was emotionally a very immature person, I think, though I had read hugely ahead of my years throughout my teens. But everything happened to me at Cambridge: I found myself as a poet, I did well in my studies, I made friends with people who have remained my friends ever since, I met and fell in love with the guy I still live with. Everything happened to me. Everything good happened to me.

Recently I read an article you wrote in 1954 about being a student at Cambridge, an article of the kind almost anyone could have written. Yet you wrote the poems that went into your first book of poems, Fighting Terms, *while you were still at Cambridge, and it really is remarkably accomplished, the poetry very mature. It's difficult tying the writer of that article and the writer of those poems together.*

I remember the article you're thinking about. It was called 'Letter from Cambridge', and it came out in the *London Magazine*. Well, poets develop earlier than prose writers. I didn't learn to write good prose until I was in my late forties. Clive Wilmer very kindly edited a collection of mine, *The Occasions of Poetry*, which was very varied. Some of it was good, some of it was quite bad, and I really thought it was time I learnt to write decent prose after that. But this is the history of literature, isn't it? A nation will learn how to write good poetry before it learns how to write good prose. Look at Elizabethan poetry, and then look at Elizabethan prose. Most of the prose is impossible.

Can you tell us something about the history of Fighting Terms, *how it came about?*

I wrote a poem at the end of my first year in Cambridge that was published by some friends of mine, people who believed in me, though they had very little reason to. It was a nice little anti-war poem that I wrote after seeing Lewis Milestone's movie, the one that came out that year: not *All Quiet on the Western Front*, but *A Walk in the Sun*. It came out in an anti-war issue of a periodical called *Cambridge Today*, and it was liked. Peter Green, who was the editor of another magazine, and who is now a famous classicist, singled it out for praise, which gave me great pleasure. It also gave me confidence, and I worked all that first summer vacation at writing poetry, and got a lot of my mistakes out of the way, I guess. I worked very hard, and very deliberately, writing a poem a week.

The poems that were included in *Fighting Terms* were written during my second and third years. The book wasn't published while I was at Cambridge, it was published a year after I'd left; but it was all undergraduate work.

Who published it?

The Fantasy Press, which was at Oxford. They had published numerous pamphlets, including one by me, which were edited by Donald Hall, a visiting American poet at Oxford. They'd gone on to publish a book of Elizabeth Jennings's poems, and then they took *Fighting Terms*.

It was Donald Hall who later encouraged you to go to the States, I believe.

He encouraged me to apply for the particular fellowship that I got in the States, which was at Stanford, since he'd had it the previous year. He was very kind to me.

Who were the most important people to you that you met at Cambridge?

Let's take them in order of meeting. There was Karl Miller, whom I met at the beginning of my second year when he was freshly up there. He became the founder of the *London Review of Books*, and has written numerous good books himself. There was Tony White, who was mainly known as an actor – he did a great deal of acting while he was at Cambridge – and who became a very close friend of mine until his death, as the result of a football accident, in his mid-forties. And there was Mike Kitay, the man I live with, an American.

I only met F.R. Leavis once, at a party, but I was very influenced by him. The interesting thing about Leavis is that he's considered such an orthodoxy now, whereas he was considered a bad boy at that time, and was not liked by the literary journalists I had mostly read up to then. He was not, probably, a very likeable person, but he had a very interesting view of literature, seeing it as a part of life. That was what was so wonderful. Literature is not like a fine wine that you taste and judge by comparison with other wines. You compare a book to a person, for example, or to an action. This was what later attracted me about another slightly difficult critic, Yvor Winters. He too considered a poem as an action. And it is, of course; it's not just a decoration.

We'll come back to Winters later. Mike Kitay was important to you intellectually, not just emotionally.

Mike is a bright man. There are five of us living in this house, and if any of us has a problem which needs talking over, he's the person who's going to help us. He has a bright, alert intelligence, which is far above mine when it comes to dealing with the daily things of life, as opposed to the more abstract things.

While I was reading your essay on Ben Jonson, I was struck by this remark, which you make in talking about one of his poems. You say, 'It is a poem of self-pity, and (in spite of all I was taught at Cambridge), self-pity is something people feel often enough for it to be a subject worth writing about.' The striking thing here is the parenthesis about Cambridge.

Yes. Anybody who took Leavis's lectures will remember the way he'd say 'self-pit-teh' when talking about, let's say, some poem by Shelley – 'Ode to the West Wind', perhaps. He thought self-pity a very bad thing to write about. I suppose it's a bad thing morally to give way to. People who are sorry for themselves are boring, aren't they? But I don't think Leavis was complaining about boringness, I think he thought self-pity was a limitation in moral fibre. He was a severe man.

Can we trace to that your more or less life-long disdain for confessional poetry?

Yes. The child was father to the man, or the young man was father to the older man, anyway. I'm not interested in confessional poetry. The closest I come to liking confessional poetry is liking Allen Ginsberg.

You were alleged to be a member of the Movement. Now we all know that the Movement didn't really exist ...

Well, I'm glad you say 'alleged'. It's such a boring subject. About six months ago, somebody introduced me before a reading, saying that I had been a member of the Movement. Well, it wasn't anything that one was a member of. I never met Philip Larkin, and I'd met very few of the others by the time the Movement is supposed to have started. People love to classify: a group of new poets came up all at once, so all of us – except Ted Hughes, who turned up a little bit later – were classed as a movement. But I'm glad to see that most people who mention me as associated with the Movement say that I'm rather different from the rest of them.

Yes, your poetry doesn't have much in common with that of Amis or Enright or Wain, or Jennings, for that matter. But there is something common to those writers, which is the desire to get away from the florid language of the New Apocalyptics, or Dylan Thomas, so in that sense you do share something with them.

I did actually admire Dylan Thomas, and still do, but a friend of mine said the other day, 'What the poets of the Movement had in common was a reaction against Dylan Thomas,' and I think that's probably right. I didn't want to write like Dylan Thomas.

The two poets I do admire from that group — and I did consent to be published in the two volumes of *New Lines*, for example, though I insisted that Ted Hughes was included in the second volume, which is not often remembered — the two poets I particularly admire are Donald Davie and Philip Larkin. Philip Larkin was an extraordinary revelation when I first read him in 1954. I can remember the anthology I read him in; I was also in that anthology. And there was a poem I really admired tremendously, called 'Wedding Wind'. It's a very Lawrentian poem, not a Larkinesque Larkin poem, and it's very good, too. The poems I like best by Larkin are those that are least like Larkin, if you see what I mean. Just the other day I was re-reading a wonderful poem called 'The Explosion' — I think it's the last poem in his last book — which is very moving, and again, it's a little bit like Lawrence, perhaps, rather than what one thinks of as Larkin — Larkin the irritable, Larkin the suburban. He's dealing much more with passions and the unironic in such poems, and I think he did it splendidly.

You say somewhere that English poets are hung-up on Larkin, meaning, I think, that his influence on them has been for the worse.

He was a wonderful poet, but a bad influence. He made people less romantic, less ready to dare, more timid. He writes so delightfully of the suburban, and of failure, and things like that, that they feel that's enough. I would like to have seen them influenced by Basil Bunting or W.S. Graham, for example. I never met either of them — by the sound of it, I was quite lucky never to have met Graham — but they were great poets, and the young would have done better to learn from them than from

Larkin (or from Hughes, for that matter).

And what about Donald Davie, the other poet you especially admired?

He became quite a close friend. Indeed, he was one of the poets I've been closest to in my life. The last time I saw him, I stayed with him and his wife in Devon. Donald and I were drinking whisky late into the night, and I found myself discussing heresy with him. I don't believe in heresy, but he was a wonderful man and could accept my atheism, as I could accept his Christianity, very well. We admired each other's work, what was individual about each other.

Despite your unwillingness to be grouped together with the Movement, was it nonetheless good for your career to be part of a group?

Undoubtedly, yes. Publicity's good for selling books, isn't it?

In a lot of people's minds, you're linked with Ted Hughes, because of the joint Selected Poems, *which a lot of people used at school. Were you friends with Hughes?*

It's very strange. We were both at Cambridge at the same time – he was a year behind me, but we overlapped for two years – and we were both writing poetry, yet I didn't meet him, I don't know why. Perhaps it was because he didn't publish anything while I was there. He only started publishing in the year after I'd left. We finally met when Faber got us together, in 1960, after the publication of my second book, and possibly his second as well. We met at lunch with my publisher, and then he asked me to have lunch with him and Sylvia Plath, who I think had just had her first child then.

And you remained friends thereafter?

Yes, yes. I liked him very much. I thought he was an admirable man, and of course an admirable poet. I was very excited by his first book, and even more excited by his second. Its tremendous energy delighted me: it was just the kind of thing I was looking for.

Did you get to know him well?

I can't say I knew him that well. I met him on quite a few occasions, and we read together once or twice. I also stayed with him overnight in Devon once. But you can't know somebody well when there's 6,000 miles between you most of the time. Even when I came back to England for a year in the mid-'60s, I didn't see that much of him. We weren't intimate friends, but you could say that we were professional friends.

It's always perplexed me that you and Ted Hughes are linked together, because you're very very different temperamentally as poets. He's the great hot-blooded poet, while the temperature of your poetry is at point-zero characteristically.

Yes, I'm a *cold* poet, aren't I? The answer to that is very easy: it was our editor Charles Monteith's idea that we should publish the joint *Selected Poems* you mentioned just now. We emerged at about the same time, and he thought that neither of us was sufficiently well-known to have his own *Selected Poems*. But a *Selected Poems* of the two of us would be ideal. Originally, his idea was to include Philip Larkin as well. Larkin was older than us and had started publishing earlier, but he didn't get well known until around that time. But yes, it was a publisher's device that associated us, that and the fact that we were both considered to be violent. Ted Hughes once said, 'Thom Gunn's is the poetry of tenderness, not violence.' I greatly appreciated that, because I think it's true.

Getting back to Fighting Terms: *how did you deal with the subject of love in the book – romantic love?*

I referred to the loved one, who was usually Mike, as 'you'. This was what Auden had always done. People say, 'Why didn't you come out of the closet, publicly, sooner than you did?' I would never have got to America, for one thing. I would never had got a teaching job, for another thing. And I would probably not have had openly homosexual poems published in magazines or books at that time, in 1954.

There was virtually nobody in Britain doing that, was there?

There weren't many in America either.

Maybe Duncan?

Duncan, definitely. He did it in 1944, outrageously and courageously.

And of course, in fiction, Baldwin and Vidal were beginning to deal with the subject. Not in '54, obviously, but Giovanni's Room *was '56.*

Yes.

Incidentally, I didn't mean to be asking you why you didn't come out earlier ...

No, but it it's an obvious question, for people with no sense of history, anyway. Of course, you're old enough to have lived through some of it, and knowledgeable enough too. But there are lots of people who aren't old enough, or who don't know enough. – Somebody we should have mentioned just now was Ginsberg.

The general readership wouldn't have known that the 'you' addressed in your poems was a man. Would your colleagues at Cambridge have known?

Oh yes. They all knew. They would invite Mike and me to parties together. Cambridge was rather different from the rest of the world. It's an interesting fact, though: I very much admired Auden's poetry while I was at Cambridge, but I didn't find out that he was queer until I came to America. It was not a commonly known fact, which seems amazing now, doesn't it? It never crossed my mind. If I'd read the early books a little more intelligently, it might have crossed my mind.

He was married, of course, which might have influenced people's perception of him.

That's true. And I did know that at the time. He did it apparently to save her from Nazi Germany.

Was 'Tamer and Hawk' one of the poems you wrote with Mike in mind?

Yes, it was. It was written really rather quickly for me. There were just a couple of drafts, and I had it. The metaphor is a very Elizabethan one, I guess, a funny thing to find in a modern poem.

> *Even in flight above*
> *I am no longer free:*
> *You seeled me with your love,*

> *I am blind to other birds –*
> *The habit of your words*
> *Has hooded me.*

I suppose they still tame hawks, I don't know.

When did you move to California?

In 1954. I crossed the Atlantic on the Queen Mary. The middle day of the three-day journey was my twenty-fifth birthday. I eventually crossed the country by train, getting off in Oakland, and arriving in San Francisco by ferry, which is a wonderful way of entering the city, a spectacular way of entering it. I came for one year, but I stayed on for – well, what would it be? – forty-five years or so.

What was behind the move to California? Was it just the offer of the fellowship?

I came to California for two reasons: to study with Yvor Winters at Stanford, but primarily to be in the same country as Mike, who'd had to go into the air-force for a couple of years, doing the equivalent of our National Service. Even though he was down in Texas, at least I was in the same country as him, and I could visit him, and him me.

You didn't start living in San Francisco right away, did you?

No, after Stanford I went down to San Antonio for a year, and taught at a small Presbyterian university called Trinity. It was the first teaching I'd ever done, and I was a really terrible teacher, didn't know anything about it. The football players who were in my freshman English class were very amused by me, and I was very amused by them, so we all got on well. But that was a year of considerable tedium, and dust storms, and other Texan things like that.

You began to write the poems included in The Sense of Movement, *some of which have very up-to-date American subject-matter – I'm thinking of 'On The Move' and 'Elvis Presley', in particular – but not yet an American tone.*

No. It's hilarious actually. I thought of doing a series of poems, based on Marvell's mower poems, about the motor cyclist. This was the year after

Marlon Brando's *The Wild One*, and the myth was just starting up. I only wrote two. One was called 'On The Move' and the other was called 'The Unsettled Motorcyclist's Vision of his Death'. There are many things to dislike about 'On the Move'. To begin with, there's the constant use of the word 'one', which I find very stilted now. Now I would use the word 'you' rather than 'one'. Then again, it's such a period piece. I say that, not because it's based on a short book by Sartre, or because it's also based on *The Wild One*, but because of its tremendous formality, which I really dislike. I'm also not sure that the last line means anything: 'One is always nearer by not keeping still.' Nearer what? Well, yes, the motorcyclist is nearer the destination, but what's the destination of human beings? Aha! It's a question that seems to answer itself but doesn't.

Yes, I was going to ask you about the line, 'It is a part solution, after all.' A part solution to what?

I don't know. There's another reason for saying that there's something wrong with the poem. It's unnecessarily well-known and anthologized.

That must be because of its subject-matter, motor-cyclists.

Yes, as though the industrial revolution had never provided subject-matter for poetry before. The other poem you mentioned was 'Elvis Presley'. He hadn't been around for long when that was first published, in 1957. He'd only been going about two years. There's only one good line in the poem, which was used by George Melly for the title of his book, *Revolt into Style*. You have to remember that that poem is about the young Elvis Presley, the Presley of 'Hound Dog' and 'Heartbreak Hotel':

> Whether he poses or is real, no cat
> Bothers to say: the pose held is a stance,
> Which, generation of the very chance
> It wars on, may be posture for combat.

And you might ask, 'Combat against what?'

The subject of The Sense of Movement *is the will, and you've said about yourself at that time that you were 'a Shakespearian, Sartrean Fascist'.*

Well, I have to make a confession to you. I didn't know, what I later learned, that 'will' in Shakespeare refers to the penis, or more generally to the sexual organs of either sex. I'd got a degree from Cambridge without ever having been informed of this fact. None of the editions of the sonnets that I used told me this. I couldn't have known it, and I don't think any of my friends knew it either, though, like a lot of people at university, I learned more from my friends than I did from my teachers. I think I was unconsciously using it for that, though, don't you? It was very much a male kind of will, a penis-like will.

Is it true to say that while the main influence on Fighting Terms *was Leavis, the main influence on* The Sense of Movement *was Winters?*

What's interesting about this is that poets aren't supposed to be influenced by critics. People used to say of Leavis that he never influenced poetry, but that's not true. He did influence my poetry. Of course, he didn't like contemporary poetry much, and if he ever read my poetry – I don't know if he did, but he might have – I shouldn't think he liked it. But Leavis and Winters were important to me, mainly because of their technical remarks. It was a wonderful thing to hear Leavis talking about the speech in *Macbeth* that goes, 'If it were done, when 'tis done, then 'twere well / It were done quickly,' commenting on the pauses and the plunges forward at the ends of the lines. He was very good when speaking about the relationship between verse movement and feeling. I didn't know anything about that kind of thing when I went up to Cambridge, so it was terrific learning about it.

As to Winters, well, of course, he was not only a teacher and critic, like Leavis, but a poet as well. He was a formidable personality – a bit *too* formidable at first. But eventually I realized there was a lot to be learned from him. He was much less rigid in conversation than he seems to be in his critical writings. One of the first things he said was, 'What, you haven't read William Carlos Williams or Wallace Stevens!? You should read them at once.' He regarded that as an essential part of my education. And of course he was right. These people's work had not been available to me in England, except maybe in anthologies. I fought Winters a lot at first. I mean, I quarrelled with him and disagreed with him. He kind of liked that. I said once, writing about him, that I felt like the rebellious soldier in the sergeant's platoon in one of those Hollywood war movies. He liked me in grim sort of way because I opposed him. I didn't really *oppose* him that much. I did *argue* with him, though. At the end of the first year, I wrote a poem called 'To Yvor Winters, 1955', and perhaps the last section of it says more about the relationship than the words I've used here. I was accused of imitating Winters's style in writing this poem, and I was: it was part of a tribute to him:

> Though night is always close, complete negation
> Ready to drop on wisdom and emotion,
> Night from the air or the carnivorous breath,
> Still it is right to know the force of death,
> And, as you do, persistent, tough in will,
> Raise from the excellent the better still.

You said that The Sense of Movement, *although it's a more sophisticated book than* Fighting Terms, *is a less independent one. Is that because of the influence of Winters?*

Oh, I didn't answer your question, did I, about Winters's influence on my second book? I think so, yes. Not that I mean to be ungrateful for it. You take influences as you can.

You say you read The Waste Land *until you were tired of it. Most young poets would then have been turning out versions of* The Waste Land, *but there's not really much influence evident of* The Waste Land *in either of your first two books.*

I read *The Waste Land* till I got tired of it. I was a child of my time, as were Philip Larkin and Ted Hughes. Larkin wasn't influenced by the Modernists, and neither was Hughes really. He started as a traditional poet, with a different kind of energy from the rest of us. You don't get the same interest in writing in fragments, which is a loose way, I guess, of speaking of Pound and Eliot. In my first year at Cambridge, I wrote a series of really dreadful poems that nobody ever saw, luckily, about old men shuffling through dead leaves. They were very Eliotian in feeling. I don't know why I wrote them. I suppose I was embodying what I thought was some kind of poetic fashion.

It wasn't Eliot who took on The Sense of Movement *at Faber, was it?*

It wasn't him personally. You know, I met him just a few months before his death. He liked to meet his authors – Faber's authors, I should say. I was very nervous – I've seldom been so nervous in anybody's company – because he was so famous, and I'd been reading him for such a long time. At one point he said, 'I haven't done the choosing of the poetry for Faber's for many years.' The disappointment must have been evident in my face, because I'd always assumed that he picked me, and he said, 'I didn't choose you, but I like your poetry very much'. He said it *very* kindly.

I don't think anything would have gone on to the list if he had particularly disliked it.

No, I don't think so either. It was actually chosen by Charles Monteith, who also chose Ted Hughes and William Golding and other people.

Let's talk about low life. 'I praise the overdogs from Alexander / To those who would not play with Stephen Spender.' You've always liked toughs, and men of action. What's the source of this fascination?

Well, probably, it's partly sexual. I'm a timid little soul myself. But an interesting thing happened in the movies, didn't it, in the early 1950s? In the '30s you had all these gentleman heroes, like Cary Grant and Leslie Howard, can you imagine! There were a few really tough guys, tough attractive guys, like Clark Gable and John Garfield. Not many though. And then, suddenly, you got this wave of people, people like Marlon Brando and James Dean. There was a new kind of ideal: it was a blue-collar hero, it wasn't the gentleman hero. There were no more scarlet pimpernels then.

Is the fascination with toughs and the like an admiration for the improvised nature of such lives? I'm thinking of the poem, 'Improvisation'.

But *he's* not a tough.

No, he's an outsider, a misfit.

And very ugly too. I think he's still around on Haight Street, poor guy. Well, the homeless I'm sorry for. They're a reproach on every corner, here, and in most big cities, I guess. It's terrible, and such a contrast with my childhood. There was the occasional tramp (or hobo as they're called here), but there were no homeless on the streets then, as there are now. Now they're there on every street. I find the same kind of fascination with outsiders in Mina Loy. Do you know her poetry?

No.

Ah, she's wonderful. I didn't start reading her work until it became available in the early '80s, by which time she'd been dead for almost twenty years. She was fascinated by all outcasts.

There's a fair amount of disguised homosexuality in The Sense of Movement.

Oh sure.

But there's some which is much more overt than might be expected. I'm thinking of 'The Beaters', for example.

That's a very unpleasant poem. I was trying to be like Baudelaire, wanting to shock people. It was bad, dishonest, poem.

That's why you left it out of your Collected Poems?

Yes, I didn't know what I was talking about.

I wonder if the book would have got past Eliot if he'd understood that poem.

Eliot had his unpleasant side, too.

What did Yvor Winters make of 'The Beaters'? Do you remember?

He didn't like it at all. He thought I was talking about the Penitentes Brotherhood – an illegal cult of some sort – which he had come across, in his youth, in New Mexico.

You said just now that you were trying to be like Baudelaire.

Yes. Baudelaire has always been a tremendous influence on me. I've always loved his poetry. I was attracted first of all by his desire to be shocking, which doesn't interest me at all now. What I have come to love are the later poems, like 'Le Cygne', or the one about the seven old men ...

'Les Sept Vieillards'.

Yes. They're wonderful, so complicatedly put together. There's a very interesting thing about the structure of poetry. You get many poems which are straightforwardly about one subject, like that elegy by John Donne, the one with the line, 'O my America! my new-found-land', where he's talking about fucking in terms of exploring a continent. I suppose most poems are straightforward in that way, but there is another kind of poem, which is even more interesting, and which seems to have been initiated by Horace. He ties together, almost arbitrarily, two completely different subjects. It's almost as though he started two different poems, and the only thing he could think of was to join them together. There are heaps of poems like this in the *Odes*. I don't know his *Satires* at all.

And there are heaps of them in Thom Gunn, poems in which you introduce one idea and then introduce, not exactly a conflicting idea, but a tangential idea.

It does marvellous things to both ideas to have them come into conflict. And Baudelaire does it too, especially in those later poems.

When did you first try to write that kind of poem? Do you remember?

I probably did it by mistake. I didn't read Horace until quite late.

There are some obvious examples later on in your work. The last poem in Jack Straw's Castle, would be one. That's two separate poems, in a way.

Yes.

'Interruption' is another. But you don't remember when you first produced a poem like that?

I have no idea. Sometimes you are working separately on two poems that won't work out, and you suddenly realize that you can connect them, that they're really the same poem, however different their subjects seemed to be. That has certainly happened to me.

One of the things that I find interesting is that, while I know you're sympathetic to a lot of the poetry of Allen Ginsberg and Kenneth Rexroth and Gary Snyder, and you were living in San Francisco, or around the Bay area, in the late '50s, you remained untouched by the poetics that the Beats were practising or exploring.

I didn't have any time for them at first. Then, a little later, I did discover Gary Snyder, whom I liked very much. I love his early work very much still, and some of the later work. Rather belatedly I came to like Ginsberg. Somebody asked me to write an article about Ginsberg for the English magazine, *The Gay Review*, and I said I would because I liked the idea of reading him all the way through. I found I loved much more of him than I expected to. What's so terrific about Ginsberg is that, even though some of the writing is very slipshod, he always makes fun of himself. Whenever he's sorry for himself, he undercuts the self-dramatization and the self-pity by making a joke of it. There's a marvellous poem of his, a fairly late one, called 'Mugging', in which he describes coming out of the place he lives in on the Lower East Side of New York — which was rougher then than it is now — and passes a group of kids, one of whom comes over and slowly puts an arm around his neck. Ginsberg says he thought at first it was an embrace, a mark of sexual affection, but it wasn't: it was an attempt to rob him of what he was carrying.

That's when he starts doing his chant, isn't it? '..."Where's the money?" /"Om Ah Hum there isn't any ..."'

That's right. But he doesn't do it loud enough, I guess, because ...

Because they mug him anyway.

That's right. It's a terrific poem — one of his best. I also like William Burroughs's novels very much. I find them engrossing, brilliant, outrageous. I can never read Jack Kerouac, though, can never read more than two pages without exasperation. I came to it too late, you know. When I was at Cambridge, I said to Mike, 'Who's this Thomas Wolfe?' And he said, 'Oh, no, you don't want to read him — you're too old already.' I was too old to read Thomas Wolfe, and I was too old to read Jack Kerouac.

But it wasn't as if you were a bespectacled little fellow, who stuck his nose in a book every night. I've seen a picture of you at time, from the cover of a record called 'On The Move' ...

Oh yes — I know it ...

You're wearing a leather jacket and tight jeans, and you're looking very much like an English boy who's come over to join the beatniks. But at the same time, when it came to poetry, you never gave up your depend-

ence on form.

I had my own ideas.

And similarly, in the '60s, while you joined in all the hippy playfulness, went in for free love and listened to the Grateful Dead, you went back at night and continued your work on the editions of Fulke Greville and Ben Jonson.

That's true. I also wrote poems about acid, but in metre.

I'll come back to that a little later. Can I ask you about Robert Duncan, who was associated with the Beats, though he wasn't one himself.

He came much earlier.

Of all those San Francisco-based poets, he was the one you admired most, and the one who had the most influence on you personally, if not poetically.

He was an amazing person. Talking with him was, by all accounts, like talking with Coleridge. He had the same tendency to talk and not stop, but he talked brilliantly, so you wanted to go on listening. I would come back from having lunch with him, and just scribble stuff in my notebook, ideas that had bubbled up in the conversation. He had a very amusing story. 'When I met Olson,' he said, 'we had immediate difficulty: we found that we both liked to talk all the time. But we solved the problem just as immediately: we *both* talked at the same time.' He was very funny about himself, and had a wonderful sense of humour. He had very wide, beautiful sympathies. He didn't like to be tied down to what his admirers thought he should be thinking. He did me a great honour once, by writing a suite of poems based on some I'd included in *Moly*. He showed them to me, and I was delighted by them, and very flattered. It was like Marlowe having written 'The Passionate Shepherd to his Love' finding Raleigh answering it. Duncan said, 'This is really going to upset my admirers; it's going to upset yours too.'

Did you like his poetry straightaway, or was it an acquired taste?

You have to select, because he published everything he wrote. The best poems are fantastic, but there's a lot that's drivel. If you want to start reading Duncan, the book to start with is *The Opening of the Field*. He would have liked you to start there too ...

'A Poem Beginning with a Line by Pindar' is one of his best, I think.

A fantastic poem, yes.

'The light foot hears you and the brightness begins.'

Yes, yes. – I didn't know what 'the light foot hears you' meant until I went back to the original, in Bowra's translation, where he explains – whether in a note or in the introduction I can't remember – that the light foot is the chorus. It's the chorus that hears it. And 'and the brightness begins' refers to the kind of euphoria that comes of being a hero in the games.

I mentioned Duncan because he's someone to whom you've dedicated several poems, and ...

And I've written three essays on him. He meant a great deal to me. Beside Winters he's probably the poet who meant most to me in my life. August Kleinzahler means a lot to me – I've learned from him certainly – but less weightily than I did from those other two. They were both overpowering people, though overpowering people of completely different sorts. I was fond of saying at one time that I was the only poet who'd dedicated poems to Yvor Winters and Robert Duncan. They didn't like each other, though they never met. Each stood for just the kind of thing the other disliked most: Winters for authority, and Duncan for anarchy, I guess (though that is unfair to both of them). Duncan was a person of tremendous generosity, with a wonderful imagination.

Wasn't the poet who had most influence on your actual practice at this time somebody who was associated with both the San Francisco writers and the Beats, the somewhat older William Carlos Williams?

Well, he'd influenced me from the late '50s onward, before I'd met any of these other people. It was Winters who got me to read him, actually.

I see your discovery of Williams as marking a complete turning-point in your writing.

I think it was.

Thinginess enters your writing at that time.

It was about time too, after all those abstractions of 'On The Move'.

The observing eye comes to life, and I've put that down, maybe wrongly, to your reading of Williams.

You're right, you're right, he was tremendously important to me. Of course, I never met him, never came close to meeting him, but he was *very* important to me. Davie hated him. He wrote possibly the most disapproving review Williams ever received, I think for the *New Republic*.

The English in general don't like Williams, can't read him.

There's no trick. Or it's the same trick as with reading Edmund Spenser. You just give yourself to him, and if you try hard enough, or wait long enough, you get it. Or else you don't get it.

The other major influence of the '60s was drugs.

Oh yes, yes. On me, and on everybody else.

How did you start taking drugs?

The first joint I ever smoked was given to me by Tony Tanner, the Cambridge don, who died in 1998. He was my great friend at the University of California, when I was starting to teach and he was a graduate student there. Everyone was taking acid in 1965, and I decided to give up tenure then. I said I wanted to devote myself to my poetry, but the real reason was that I wanted to go to concerts in the park and take acid. I wasn't going to take acid until I'd stopped teaching, because I thought there might be some hangover effect. I did quite a bit of it with all my friends in the next few years. It gave me all sorts of subject-matter.

The '60s was a relatively quiet decade for you, in terms of writing poetry.

Yes, I was having great difficulty writing in the early '60s. I wondered whether I wasn't stopping writing altogether, because the poems were so few and came with such difficulty. And then, when I started taking acid — which we did an *awful* lot of — I was thirty-five by then — not a youngster — it was wonderful. It got rid of all your fixed notions, and stirred you up, and you got wonderful visual images. This hadn't been my intention. When I've started on a series of poems, like the ones about acid, I've never known it was going to be a series. The poems have just come to me, one by one, until I suddenly found that there was a continuing theme.

There's a change in your poetry at about the time of Moly, *with the introduction of more humanity, more tenderness — something which continues to inform your later poetry. Is this something you would put down to your drug experience?*

It would be nice to, but I don't know.

But were you aware of the drugs opening up sides of yourself, which hitherto ...

It's a difficult question to answer. *Maybe* the drug-taking made me a nicer person. But you know, I was more assured as a person, and when you're surer of yourself, you're nicer to others, because you're having it easier. When you're unsure of yourself, you're very pushy and intolerant of others. — Allen Ginsberg said he went through tremendous psychic change because of taking acid. We all *hoped* for that, and thought that's what we were undergoing at the time. But I'm a little more sceptical about it now.

You don't take acid any longer?

If somebody offered it to me, I would probably take it, yes. But it's not that easy to come by. And what we used to take in the '60s was *so strong*. What I've had since then has been, oh, good for sexual play, but very mild. It used to be quite difficult getting up there, but once you got there, once you were peaking, that was great, and you'd start to come down and it was just wonderful from then on. The first stages could be quite difficult, but we never talked about that — we said it was all good.

I haven't taken acid for years. I used to take a lot too.

Well, you know what I mean, then.

One of the poems in Moly *that's bound up with your drug experiences is 'Street Song':*

> I am too young to grow a beard
> But yes man it was me you heard
> In dirty denim and dark glasses.
> I look through everyone who passes
> But ask him clear, I do not plead,
> Keys lids acid and speed.

Yes, I'd been struck by all the people, mainly young men, rambling around the streets of San Francisco at that time, advertising drugs and selling them. (Probably the same was happening on the streets of New York, London and Paris. Who knows?) They would pass you and say, 'Want to buy any acid, speed, buds?', and I was put in mind of Elizabethan street songs – you know: open markets, people carrying their wares on trays round their necks, calling out things like, 'Cherry ripe, cherry ripe' – the street cries of London. 'Street Song' was about the street cries of San Francisco. *Keys,* incidentally, were kilos of marijuana, and *lids* were ounces. The other two speak for themselves.

Was there something deliberate about choosing metre to express the drug experiences?

No, I don't think it was a conscious decision. It's very seldom a conscious decision whether I write in metre or free verse. It just seems to come out that way in early drafts of the poem, and I feel happy to go on with it if it seems to be working. Later on I realized what I was doing: I was filtering the experiences of the infinite through the grid of the finite. I wrote about this somewhere, and compared it to what Thomas Mann was doing in *Doctor Faustus.* Mann said he'd had to filter the character of the genius-composer Adrian Leverkühn through the bourgeois consciousness of his narrator, Serenus Zeitblom.

Do you find it in general helps you to keep a rein on your subject matter when you employ metre? Is it a way of restraining personal anarchy?

I'm never in danger of personal anarchy – I'm terribly well-controlled. I don't like that aspect of myself very much. I'm not a very spontaneous kind of person: I'm cautious and deliberate, and I usually know what I'm doing, except when I'm just being stupid. I'm not Heathcliff. It would be nice to be Heathcliff, but I'm not. At least, I *think* it would be nice to be Heathcliff.

Not all of the poems in Moly *are about drugs, of course. One I particularly like is 'Apartment Cats', which has a very tender, domestic, quality: 'The Girls wake, stretch, and pad up to the door. / They rub my leg and purr.'*

I lived with Mike for ten years in an apartment in North Beach, and we had two cats there, called Fletcher and Black. It was the sort of apartment that's called a 'railroad apartment' because it's like the corridor of a railroad carriage – or car, as we say here – with all of the rooms coming off it. The cats used to go wild every now and then, and they'd run up and down that corridor

One thing that you like to do, particularly in the books since Moly, *is to populate a book with local types and local streets. You like to record a scene, don't you?*

Yes, yes, I like to tell stories, I like to record a scene, things that I come across in my life. I hide them away sometimes, like little secrets that other people might not recognize.

Are these scenes things you've jotted down in your notebooks?

I suppose so, but I don't quarry the notebooks for details while I'm writing a poem, not usually, anyway. The process of writing is what generates the details. I love what Pound said about Hardy's poetry. He said he liked it so much because Hardy concentrated on the subject matter above technique. Technique just followed. That's the way a writer should go: you should be obsessed with your subject, and by being faithful to your subject, all the rest should follow.

One of the poems in which you record a scene – it's one I particularly like – is 'All Do Not All Things Well'.

That's about two of my neighbours in the early 1970s, who liked to mend cars. I didn't write the poem till about twelve years after they left, evicted because they were running a business on the street:

I am sorry that they went.
Quick with a friendly greeting,
They were gentle joky men
– Certainly not ambitious,
Perhaps not intelligent
Unless about a car,
Their work one thing they knew
They could for certain do
With a disinterest
And passionate expertise
To which they gave their best
Desires and energies

The title, which is also the first line, comes from a song by Thomas Campion, written at the turn of the 16th and 17th centuries. It's a wonderful song, much anthologized, which begins 'Now winter nights enlarge / The number of their hours', and it's about the winter pastimes in the great house in Elizabethan times. The four lines from which the title comes go: 'All do not all things well, / Some measures comely tread, / Some knotted riddles tell, / Some poems smoothly read.' If ever I read 'All Do Not All Things Well', I have to point out that when I use the word 'disinterested', I do not mean 'lack of interest', I mean 'impartiality'. You'd be surprised what the dictionaries say nowadays. Following new usage, they say that 'lack of interest' is one of the word's meanings. (Good Lord! I'll be dead soon. I don't need to live in this new world.)

How long does it usually take you to write a poem?

It can vary between a couple of days and a year. When I say a year, I don't mean that I work at it every day. I'll set on one side something that isn't finished but which I can't take any further, and then come back to it from time to time. Sometimes you find out how to carry on if you just let it rest for a while.

So you don't find any virtue in Ginsberg's insistence on spontaneous composition?

I find it hard to believe people who say they never revise. Robert Duncan used to insist that he never revised, and I'd say, 'But look at the difference between this published version of the poem and that one.' And he'd say, 'Oh I *altered some bits*, of course, but I don't *revise*.' Robert

Graves used to say that he didn't revise, and maybe that was true. Myself, I can't conceive of doing without revision. Occasionally a poem has come out almost on first draft, but there are always a few alterations I have to make.

Do you ever feel you've squeezed the life out of a poem, by making revisions?

Certainly. That has happened.

Your muse is an urban muse, on the whole. But I've got you down as a nature poet as well, not in the generally accepted sense, perhaps, but a lot of your poems strike me as being about the very stirrings of life. I find it remarkable how often you return to that subject.

That's interesting. I would have thought mine was a suburban muse, a bit like Keats's. You know they called Keats a Cockney poet, I think because he wasn't a Lake poet, was only interested in Hampstead Heath. Of course, Hampstead Heath was more like real country then, not like it is now.

I'm thinking of poems like 'A Kind of Ethics', or 'The Cherry Tree'. They're about the very moment at which the sap begins to rise:

> But there's something going on
> in those twisted brown limbs,
> it starts as a need
> and it takes over, a need
> to push
>   push outward
> from the centre, to
> bring what is not
> from what is, pushing
> till at the tips of the push
> something comes about
>   and then
> pulling it from outside
> until yes she has them started
> tiny bumps
> appear at the end of twigs.

Sure, but these are often about things that happen in gardens or parks, rather than real countryside.

Where does 'The Cherry Tree' come from?

I was staying with one of my many aunts, in a village near Sittingbourne in Kent. The cherry tree was in the next garden, and I would see it all loaded with blossom from my bedroom window. The poem follows the cherry tree through twelve months, so it ends at its beginning, in a sense. But as a matter of fact, that poem is quite as much about a female cat that I had, and about her having kittens. I was struck by the fact that she was so enormously attached to them at first, but that, after a while, when they were getting out on their own, and she'd be sitting at a distance, she'd become more and more indifferent to them. She cared nothing about her offspring at that point. So it's as much about my cat as it was about the cherry tree.

There's another strand in your work, which involves the poet being in the dark and asking how he knows he exists. There are a lot of poems about that. I think 'Touch' is one.

I was very pleased with 'Touch' because it was the first poem, I think, where I really felt I was writing decent free verse that had interesting rhythms:

> What I, now loosened,
> sink into is an old
> big place, it is
> there already, for
> you are already
> there, and the cat
> got there before you, yet
> it is hard to locate.

You have to understand that it's very difficult changing from metre to free verse after you've been writing in metre for the previous ten years or so. When I started writing in England in the late '40s and early '50s, I did what was fashionable. I thought I was being independent, but actually I was just imitating what other people were doing, which was writing in metre and rhyme. Then I came over to America and I discovered the works of the Modernists, who weren't in print in England when I left, in

1954, amazing as that is to realize. Wallace Stevens's *Selected Poems* was published for the first time by Faber in 1954, the year I left. William Carlos Williams was not available anywhere. I wanted to write free verse, but it's not that easy suddenly changing. It's very difficult getting that iambic thump out of your ear. And so I invented a way for myself: I wrote syllabics. Other people had written syllabics before, but not many. There was Marianne Moore, of course, though her syllabics were very eccentric ones which you would probably have mistaken for free verse unless you did a count. There was also Robert Bridges, who experimented with a very long syllabic line. But the person whose syllabics were of greatest interest to me was my old friend Donald Hall. He'd been experimenting with a shorter line and I was struck by how good some of his poems in that form were. Anyway, using syllabics was a way of teaching myself free verse rhythms.

Am I right in thinking that 'My Sad Captains' was one of your earliest syllabic poems?

Yes. 'My Sad Captains' was one of the first. It uses a seven-syllable line, and I think it came out quite well.

> One by one they appear in
> the darkness: a few friends, and
> a few with historical
> names. How late they start to shine!

People ask me who My Sad Captains were, are. Nowadays we would call them 'mentors', I guess, but they're also our dead heroes and teachers. The phrase comes from *Antony and Cleopatra*, of course.

You haven't used syllabics for a while?

I haven't written syllabics in many years now, but they were very useful to me then.

You seemed at first to approach free verse with Frost's remark in mind, about playing tennis without a net.

I don't agree with that. No, I don't think poetry is a game of tennis. Free verse has to contain rhythms as interesting as those in metrical verse. It means having to improvise each line, so it's that much more difficult to write competent free verse than to write competent metrical verse, because with metre you always have the basic paradigm to fall back on.

Yours is still a short line, isn't it, when you write free verse?

You know where I get it from? I get my whole attraction to free verse from reading William Carlos Williams, and he used a short line, some people say because he wrote so many of his poems on prescription pads after his day's work as a doctor was over. I should add, perhaps, that I find it easier to write a good short free verse line than a long free verse line, just because it tends to be less prosy.

Did the move from metre to free verse change the way you thought? Because you'd actually been thinking in metre.

You're asking about things I wasn't conscious of. Looking back on it, I suppose it did, yes. Free verse has a tendency to suggest the improvisatory. D.H. Lawrence wrote a very interesting essay about this, which is usually printed under the title of 'Poetry of the Present'.

Are unpredictable meanings more likely to creep into the more loosely structured poems, would you say?

Perhaps, but I'd say that what makes any poem good is what's been improvised while you've been working on it, as opposed to what you already had planned, if anything. It's not going to be a very interesting poem if all it contains is what you planned to write beforehand.

For me, another most appealing characteristic of your poetry is the lack of rhetoric, the lack of easy rhetoric. I always feel when I'm reading your poetry that nothing has been gained easily. You have had to work hard for every phrase, and it never just takes flight into easy rhetoric.

I distrust myself with rhetoric, because it would be a form of falsification. Though I adore writers like Milton and Yeats, and even Lowell at times, they are writers of rhetoric, and not my kind of writer. I feel much closer to someone who's become alarmingly fashionable in the last few years, Elizabeth Bishop, who was very much against rhetoric. I wrote an essay about that, reviewing a very good book by David Kalstone called *Becoming a Poet*. She speaks about her difficulties with Lowell's work, which at times, in a sense, falsified things. She disapproved of that. She, having learned from Marianne Moore, wants the literal truth much more. I find that more difficult and more desirable too. If I were a rhetorical poet, once I let myself start lying like that I'd lie in all sorts of different directions. I'd be appalling. I may be appalling anyway, but not in that way.

So when you sense a rhetorical flourish creeping in, do you banish it quickly?

I try to, yes. Though we all have our little effects, don't we, for trying to say things well?

But there's very seldom a cheap rhetorical flourish in a Thom Gunn poem.

Is a rhetorical flourish in Milton cheap? It seems to me that it's magnificent, even if it is rhetoric.

Milton no. You're taking me to an extreme there. But I would say that rhetorical flourishes in Ted Hughes are sometimes cheap.

Sure, I agree. But compare Milton with Herbert, for example, or Bishop with Lowell. Herbert is a minor poet when compared with Milton, and Bishop is a minor poet when compared with Lowell.

I'd like to ask you one more question about metre. When you're writing a metrical poem, do you choose a model which you think is suited to the subject you've started out with?

I don't remember doing so. Maybe once or twice. I just write it down, and if the first stanza comes out nicely then I carry on. I don't think I've ever done what Yeats did when he wrote 'In Memory of Major Robert Gregory', where he deliberately imitated the form of a memorial poem by Cowley. There's a mixture of deliberateness and undeliberateness in the early stages of writing, I think. You write down what you can. If it comes out looking nice on the page, you carry on, and if it doesn't, you try something else.

Do you have dry periods, when you don't write very much?

Yes. Doesn't everybody? Oh yes, they're terrible, especially after finishing a book. And it gets longer after every book. After *Jack Straw's Castle*, I didn't write a thing for two-and-a-half years, or never *finished* a thing anyway. I wrote industriously in my notebook, but nothing came out of it. I really thought that this was probably the end, you know? People often stop writing long before they die. I remember saying to a friend of mine, 'It probably doesn't matter, but I don't think I'll write any more poetry,' and he said, very sweetly, 'Well, it matters to me, and I hope you do come back to writing.' I did come back to it, of course, and in the most peculiar way, which was very charming. I was teaching at the University of California, Davis, just for one term. They'd asked me to fill in for somebody else. I was teaching a creative writing class, and there was one boy in it whose two passions were poetry and baseball. His name was John Caire, and he was so good: he worked hard, and improved with every poem he wrote. He wrote about one poem a week for the whole term, which was ten weeks long. It was very nice to watch him; it reminded me of myself when I was at that stage of my life. And I was excited by this, and I thought, 'Well, I can do that kind of thing, can't I?' He was writing a narrow kind of poem that he'd originally learnt from Philip Levine, who came from his home town, Fresno, and I thought, 'I can write that kind of thing.' And I did: I started writing again.

How do you know when a book is finished? Take Boss Cupid, *for example: how did you know that that was finished?*

I don't know. When you've accumulated a few poems, over the space of a few years, you have a sense that something has been covered, though you don't always rationalize it. I'll give you an interesting example. *The Man with Night Sweats* was published in 1992, and Hugh Haughton wrote a terrific review of it which appeared in the *TLS*. Haughton said that there was an image of embracing running right the way through the book, but when I read that I thought, '*Is* there?' So I went through the book, and he was absolutely right: in almost every poem there is an image of embracing. I hadn't realized this until I read Haughton's review, long after the book was published. Usually, when you have an accumulation of poems, you can see that something has been covered. You haven't had any intention of covering a subject or a theme – you don't think in such abstract terms – but the human mind is concerned with certain things at certain times, and the poems reflect that. You know, when I was reading Caroline Spurgeon, while studying Shakespeare at the university, I remember wondering whether Shakespeare really knew what he was doing at every point. When in *Macbeth* he brings in the image of the dwarf wearing the giant's clothes, or wearing robes that are too loose, and stuff like that, did he think, 'We haven't brought in this image for some scenes, so let's get it in here'? Of course he didn't: it's just that his mind was consistent. Anybody's mind has its consistencies like that.

The Man with Night Sweats is a book composed largely, though not entirely, of elegies. Can you say something about the title poem?

It is spoken by somebody who wakes sweating and assumes that he has AIDS. I am lucky enough not to be HIV positive, but in those early years, when it seemed so mysterious, and so especially nightmarish, and when people that I knew were dying, or had already died ... If you sweat during the night, maybe you just have flu, or maybe you just have too many blankets on, but you think: 'Oh my God, this is night sweats,' the night sweats that precede AIDS:

> I wake up cold, I who
> Prospered through dreams of heat
> Wake to their residue,
> Sweat, and a clinging sheet.

A friend of mine pointed out, after the poem was completed, that it's got echoes of a technique employed by Marvell in 'An Horatian Ode upon Cromwell's Return from Ireland'. My short couplets are a little like the ones you find in that poem, and I'm sure that Marvell's tune must have been swimming around in my memory – the memory of my ear – without my being conscious of it. Sometimes I've woken up in the morning with the intonation of a line of poetry in my ear, a line it can take me a day or two to track down. Once it was a line from *Pericles:* 'A terrible child-bed hast thou had, my dear'. It's an extraordinary little tune that line has. Then there were two lines from Tennyson's 'To the Reverend F.D. Maurice': 'And only hear the magpie gossip / Garrulous under a roof of pine.'

And these tunes sometimes find a way into your own poems, but not consciously?

Yes.

A number of the elegies in The Man with Night Sweats *are written in couplets. The title poem isn't uniformly in couplets, I know, but it does employ them at intervals ...*

Yes, in that poem you have a short quatrain followed by a couplet, which I keep to fairly consistently, though you might not notice that from hearing it.

But 'The J Car', for example, is straight couplets. And there are others. Did you decide to use couplets like this, or did it just happen that way?

It just happened that way. But it's interesting you should mention 'The J Car' here, because there is a deliberate steal in there. I took the first of its last four lines from the ghost in *Hamlet*, who says 'Unhouseled, disappointed, unaneled.' I thought that was too good a line not to copy:

> Unready, disappointed, unachieved,
> He knew he would not write the much-conceived
> Much-hoped-for work now, nor yet help create
> A love he might in full reciprocate.

Charlie, to whom 'The J Car' is addressed, wrote poetry, and even wrote a novel. The novel wasn't up to much, but the poetry was really quite good. He was new to it, of course; he was very young; he died at the age of thirty.

Were you troubled by survival guilt?

Yes, everybody was, everybody who had friends who were dying. You felt, 'Why not me?' You know, I had run around, and had had sex in various forms of extraordinary risk in the late '70s, just when everybody was starting to get infected. I wrote a poem called 'Courtesies of the Interregnum' – it's another of the ones employing couplets – in which I talk about going to see a friend of mine in New York, somebody I knew very well, who was HIV positive:

> He is, confronted by a guest so fit,
> Almost concerned lest I feel out of it,
> Excluded from the invitation list
> To the largest gathering of the decade, missed
> From membership as if the club were full.

> It is not that I am not eligible,
> He gallantly implies ...

He was trying to make me feel so much at ease: it wasn't my fault that I wasn't infected; I was really just as good, or just as attractive, as the people who were infected. It was very sweet of him.

I wonder if you were the first poet really to tackle the subject of AIDS?

I don't think so, though I don't know who was. But it became as obligatory a subject for poetry by the mid-'80s, and right up to the present day, as the war in Vietnam was in its time. And it has produced just as much bad poetry.

The book was published in 1992, I know, but when had you started writing the poems?

I can tell you exactly: I started writing them in 1984, and I finished in 1988.

Would it be fair to say that 'A Sketch of the Great Dejection' is the gravitational centre of the book?

No. I tell you, when I was putting this book together, I could see how the poems in the first part went together – that was like *Timber* in Ben Jonson's *Collected Poetry*, where I find the stately poems, the more formal poems, the more ambitious poems – and I could see how, certainly, the AIDS poems went into the last section. And then I could see how all of the other poems, except one, went very well into a more miscellaneous third section. But what to do with this poem that didn't seem to belong with anything at all? I made a section for it all by itself. That was desperation. I'm not sure it belongs there, but I like the poem and I wanted to get it in the book. But that's just my opinion. You're the observer, and may know more about me than I do.

It does reflect the themes of the book, in the sense of being a poem about sickness and recuperation.

Not *sickness* and recuperation: *adolescence* and recuperation. Obviously there's a bit of Bunyan in there – you know: life is a journey. Not a very uncommon metaphor. Not *at all* an uncommon metaphor. And there is a memory of the marshes in the north of Kent. There is also quite a bit that is really stolen from the beginning of *Great Expectations*, where Pip goes into the churchyard. I knew that churchyard, it's at Cooling. You know, with the little graves of all the children? My uncle was the village schoolmaster in All Hallows, which is quite close to there. I put an allegorical self into that landscape, and exaggerated it a bit. 'A Sketch of the Great Dejection' – the literal meaning of 'dejection' in Latin is: *thrown down*. It's the dejection of adolescence that we all go through. Donald Davie was interested in the fact that I used some very Biblical language in that poem.

> My body insisted on restlessness
> > having been promised love,
> as my mind insisted on words
> > having been promised the imagination.
> So I remained alert, confused, uncomforted.

But I also used such terms as 'I fared on', and stuff like that. He wondered how I, not a Christian, could use such language. He didn't remember that I went to school in England, where we had readings from the Bible every day. I knew the Bible very well – *know* the Bible very well.

I still think that poem is the gravitational centre of the book.

Well, maybe.

I asked you earlier why you came to the US. If I'd asked you why you left England, would I have got a different answer?

I don't know why I left England. I don't know why I'm so happy not living there. But I don't like the self I was in England very much, I guess. I figure, if I changed myself when I went to the university, then I changed myself again when I came here. We have these delusions, don't we, that we change ourselves? And sometimes we change our names when we do it. I was very interested to learn that my mother, who was born Ann-Charlotte Thomson, was known as Nancy all through her childhood, became Nan when she was first married, and then, when she was divorced, became Ann-Charlotte. Later on, at the end of her life, she became just Charlotte. I wonder whether she was aware that she was marking a different personality in each case? I don't think so. I wasn't aware of it in my own case, not until long after I'd made the change.

Are you aware of a different personality in Thom Gunn the English poet and Thom Gunn the American poet?

Probably. I feel now that I'm almost American, even though I'm still British by nationality. I don't think nationality matters that much. It's a symbol of something, but not of anything I'm interested in, I think.

You said you were fond of the appellation, 'Anglo-American poet'. Are you the only member of this species?

No, I don't think so. Auden was an Anglo-American poet, wasn't he? He had the strangest accent, though ...

What was so strange about it?

Well, it was the accent of someone who'd been to an English public school, impeccable, pure, in every respect but one: the short *as*. I remember him talking about the audience's reaction to Baba the Turk in the opera he did with Stravinksy, *The Rake's Progress*. He said, not 'The audience laughed', but 'The audience laffed'. It was very funny: you'd get these short *as* in the middle of what was otherwise impeccably upper-class English speech.

Are there any other Anglo-Americans?

The writer I think I modelled myself on, always tried to model myself on after I met him, was Isherwood.

In the sense that he had successfully transplanted himself from England to America?

Yes.

But the transplantation hasn't been a vexing experience for you in any way, has it?

No. I've had a very lucky life. Since about the age of twenty, I've had nothing but good luck. I've been amazingly lucky. I'm sure to die of some terrible, wasting disease, just to make up for it all.

Do you never miss the oldness of Europe at all?

No, I find plenty to be interested in here in San Francisco, and in New York when I go there.

But a lot of your poems have subjects that draw on Europe's distant past, the classical period, the renaissance. You don't miss that texture in your life?

It's an interesting question, whether I miss Europe. Not much, no. If I missed it that much, I'd go back there, or go back more often. I take it with me, I guess.

In the new book, Boss Cupid, *you've got a series of poems about Jeffrey Dahmer, the serial cannibalistic killer. They're bound to raise a few eyebrows, I think. Can you tell me where they came from?*

When I wrote these poems, I thought I was just doing the sort of thing Shakespeare did with *Macbeth*, another serial murderer. I've been surprised by the way people have been so shocked by them. I read all five poems, or songs – I thought of them as songs – at the beginning of a reading in Chicago a couple of years ago, and when I read the last of them, still only about twelve minutes into the hour, a group of about seven middle-aged or old ladies all rose together and made to leave. I addressed their backs as they were retreating: 'Ladies, I'm very sorry to have upset you, but Jeffrey Dahmer didn't kill nearly so many people as Napoleon or Julius Caesar, and you wouldn't have minded if I'd written poems about either of them, would you?' They didn't turn, and didn't answer. I think my final words were, 'Dahmer at least enjoyed the dead bodies after he'd killed them.'

Hah!

I wrote those poems after seeing a long review by Patricia Highsmith of two books about Jeffrey Dahmer, where she very succinctly laid out all the events of Dahmer's life. I couldn't get hold of the books over here, since they were presumably published in England, but eventually I realized that I didn't need them, because I'd got enough facts already, from that review. It was an admirable article.

It was in the TLS, *I think.*

It was, yes. 'Hitchhiker' is the first poem of the sequence, which eventually contained five, all spoken by Jeffrey Dahmer himself. Or perhaps I should say *sung* by him, because I thought of them as songs. 'Hitchhiker' concerns the first murder that he committed, at the age of 18 or 19. He was out driving, and picked up a hitchhiker, a guy called Steve, I think, who was on his way to see his girlfriend. Steve had long blond hair going down his back, and a bare chest, and for Jeffrey Dahmer the chest was the best feature in the human male. He never carried it out, but later on he even conceived the idea of constructing an altar out of the skeleton of a human chest, putting candles at different corners of it. So, Dahmer, who was staying by himself in his parents' house, asked the guy to come back for a beer and a joint. Steve came back for the beer but refused the joint, and was about to go when Dahmer was suddenly struck by the horrified realization that he'd fallen deeply in love with somebody – it had been love at first sight – and he was never going to see him again. So he did the obvious thing, came up behind him, pressed a dumbbell against Steve's throat and choked him to death.

> Oh do not leave me now,
> All that I ever wanted is compressed
> In your sole body. As you turn to go
> I know that I must keep you, and know how,
> For I must hold the ribbed arch of your chest
> And taste your boyish glow.

The poem tries to sound like an Elizabethan love poem.

And the general title of the sequence, 'Troubadour'?

Well, the troubadours sang for love without getting much in the way of recompense for their romantic feelings.

You said to me the other afternoon, while we were getting happily drunk in Vesuvio's, that one should always be happy to be the age one is. You seem remarkably cheerful approaching 70.

Hah! I don't remember saying that, but I certainly think it. I'm leading the life I want to live, and I don't have anything much to regret, I guess.

When are you going to give up teaching?

When the term stops, in May 1999. And the day I retire I will send off the manuscript of *Boss Cupid,* and that will mean there is still something left to live for: publication of this book.

Are you anticipating another dry spell after that?

I didn't write very many poems last year. I only wrote about five.

Was 'Painting by Vuillard' one of those?

Yes it was. I wrote that in Washington, a city that contains numerous colossal art galleries, so many that you could spend ten days there and still only see a small part of what they have. Anyway, I had an hour to spare, so I thought I'd just wander into a gallery and spend the time looking at pictures. One of the rooms I went into – Twentieth-Century French, I guess – contained a picture by Vuillard that I was very attracted by. It was an oil painting on cardboard, and showed two old women drinking coffee.

You contrast these two old women, who are 'as brown as coffee', with the elderly people you see as you come out of the gallery. They

>   are not browned, not in the least,
> But if they do not look like coffee they look
> As pungent and startling as good strong coffee tastes,
> Possibly mixed with chicory. And no cream.

It was obviously rather quickly done, almost a caricature, in fact.

I want to close by quoting something you wrote about Gary Snyder: 'He does the real thing. He writes poetry, and like most serious poets he is concerned at finding himself on a barely known planet, in an almost unknown universe, where he must attempt to create and discover meanings.' That's Thom Gunn describing Thom Gunn, isn't it?

I expect so.

≡

Clean Clothes:
a soldier's song

When you first look at me
It is my clothes you see
Filled out – but full
Of crisp romantic otherness
Free even of smell unless,
Faint from the quartermaster, of a world of wool.

But wool, synthetics, cloth,
Though guarded from the moth,
Soon darken, wet
At crotch and collar, ankles too,
From all that I go through:
Heat and humiliation grease them with my sweat.

And now that smell I hate:
The human concentrate,
The personal,
Rises, a reek already stale,
Muddled and young and male,
My body stewing in its close-fit casserole.

How else then could I stay
Adequate day by day
Drenching each crease,
Without the thought of change into
Dry clean clothes that renew
The anonymity which holds me in one piece?

So after bath or shower,
For fully the first hour
They touch my skin
Like cool hands in a park at night
Impersonal and light
Withholding me from self, and regiment, and kin.

Thom Gunn

Bibliography

This bibliography combines information gleaned from the following sources: Jack W.C. Hagstrom and George Bixby's *Thom Gunn: A Bibliography, 1940-1978*, Jack W.C. Hagstrom and Joshua Odell's five articles, 'Emendations to *Thom Gunn: A Bibliography, 1940-1978'*, I-V (publication details are given on p. 101 below) and Jack W.C. Hagstrom's more recent unpublished notes. Certain departures from the form and content of Hagstrom *et al*'s work should be noted, however: (1) limitations on space have obliged us to omit some of the material they include (Juvenilia, Letters to Newspapers and Journals, Responses to Questionnaires, Radio and TV appearances [except where these have been recorded and/or transcribed], and Book Endorsements); (2) the same limitations have also obliged us to leave out most of the descriptive data they record (i.e. data relating collations, bindings, dimensions, print runs, prices, etc); (3) items not listed by Hagstrom *et al*, but found in various periodicals indexes – they are almost exclusively post 1995 – have been added; (4) Hagstrom *et al*'s numbering system has been dispensed with, so as to allow a certain amount of re-ordering.

Primary Works

Books, Pamphlets and Broadsides

Thom Gunn (The Fantasy Poets, 16), Fantasy Press, Oxon, p/b, 1953.
Fighting Terms, Fantasy Press, Oxon, h/b, 1954 / Hawk's Well Press, New York, h/b, 1958 / Faber, London, h/b, 1962; p/b, 1970.
Fighting Terms: a Selection, Bancroft Library Press, University of California, California, p/b, 1983.
The Sense of Movement, Faber, London, h/b, 1957; p/b, 1968 / University of Chicago Press, Illinois, h/b, 1959.
My Sad Captains and Other Poems, Faber, London, h/b, 1961; p/b, 1974/ University of Chicago Press, Illinois, h/b + p/b, 1961.
Selected Poems by Thom Gunn and Ted Hughes, Faber, London, p/b, 1962.
A Geography, Stone Wall Press, Iowa City, p/b, 1966.
Positives (with photographs by Ander Gunn), Faber, London, h/b, 1966; p/b, 1973 / University of Chicago Press, Illinois, h/b, 1967.
Touch, Faber, London, h/b, 1967; p/b, 1974 / University of Chicago Press, Illinois, h/b, 1968; p/b, 1968.
The Garden of the Gods, Pym-Randall Press, Cambridge, Massachusetts, p/b, 1968.
The Explorers, Richard Gilbertson, Crediton, Devon, h/b, p/b, 1969.
The Fair in the Woods (Sycamore Broadside, 6), Sycamore Press, Oxford, p/b, 1969.
Poems 1950-1966: A Selection, Faber, London, p/b, 1969.
Sunlight, Albondocani Press, New York, p/b, 1969.
My Sad Captains (broadside), Edward Phelps, 1970; 1977.
Moly, Faber, London, h/b, 1971; p/b, 1987.
Moly and *My Sad Captains*, Farrar, Straus and Giroux, New York, h/b + p/b, 1973.
Last Days at Teddington (broadside), Poem-of-the-Month Club, London, 1971.
Poem after Chaucer, Albondocani Press and Ampersand Books, New York, p/b, 1971.
The Spell (broadside), Nina Carroll, Northants, 1973.
Songbook, Albondocani Press, New York, p/b, 1973.
To the Air, David R. Godine, Boston, Massachusetts, h/b, 1974.
Mandrakes (illustrated by Leonard Baskin), The Rainbow Press, h/b, 1974.
Jack Straw's Castle, Frank Hallman, New York, p/b, 1975; h/b, 1976.

The Missed Beat (with an illustration by Simon Brett), The Janus Press, Newark, Vermont, h/b, 1976 / The Gruffyground Press, 1976.
Jack Straw's Castle and Other Poems, Faber, London, h/b + p/b, 1976 / Farrar, Straus and Giroux, New York, h/b, 1976; p/b, 1977.
A Crab (leaflet), anonymously published, 1978.
Bally Power Play (illustrated by Mary Harman), (unbound pamphlet), The Massey Press, Toronto, 1979.
Games of Chance (illustrated by John Thein), Abattoir Editions, Omaha, Nebraska, 1979.
Selected Poems: 1950-1975, Faber, London, h/b + p/b, 1979 / Farrar, Straus and Giroux, New York, h/b + p/b, 1979.
A Waking Dream (broadside), Victoria Press, Gravesend, Kent, 1980.
Talbot Road, Helicon Press, New York, p/b, 1981.
The Menace (illustrated by J.J. Hazard), Manroot, San Francisco, California, p/b, 1982.
The Passages of Joy, Faber, London, h/b + p/b, 1982 / Farrar, Straus and Giroux, New York, h/b + p/b, 1982.
The Occasions of Poetry, Faber, London, h/b, 1982.
The Occasions of Poetry: Essays in Criticism and Autobiography, an expanded edition, North Point Press, San Francisco, California, p/b, 1985.
Well Dennis O'Grady (broadside), Streetfare Journal, Winston Network, Mill Valley, California, 1984.
Sidewalks (illustrated by Bill Schuessler), Albondocani Press, New York, p/b, 1985.
The Hurtless Trees (illustrated by Andrew Hudson), Jordan Davies, New York, p/b, 1986.
Lament (illustrated by Bill Schuessler), Doe Press, Champaign, Illinois, h/b + p/b, 1985.
Night Sweats, Robert L. Barth, Florence, Kentucky, p/b, 1987.
Undesirables, Pig Press, Durham, p/b, 1988.
Death's Door, Red Hydra Press, Tuscaloose, Alabama, h/b, 1989.
At the Barriers, Nadja, New York, h/b + p/b, 1989.
Jamesian (broadside), Robert L. Barth, Florence, Kentucky, 1990.
Thomas Bewick (broadside), Eucalyptus Press, Mills College, 1990.
My Mother's Pride (broadside), Dia, New York, 1990.
The Life of the Otter (broadside), Carroll's Books, San Francisco, California, 1990.
The Man with Night Sweats, Faber, London, h/b + p/b, 1992 / Farrar, Straus and Giroux, New York, h/b, 1992.
The Man with Night Sweats (broadside), Black Oak Books, Berkeley, California, 1992.
Old Stories, Sea Cliff Press, New York, p/b, 1992.
The Last Poem (broadside), Unterberg Poetry Center of the 92nd Street Y, New York, 1992.
Saturday Night (broadside), Turret Bookshop, London, 1992.
Untitled (broadside), Black Oak Books, Berkeley, California, 1993.
Shelf Life: Essays, Memoirs and an Interview, University of Michigan Press, Ann Arbor, MI, h/b + p/b 1993 / Faber, London, h/b, 1994; p/b, 1996.
Unsought Intimacies (illustrations by Theophillus Brown), Peter Koch, Berkeley, California, h/b, 1994.
Collected Poems, Faber, London, h/b, 1993; p/b, 1994 / Farrar, Straus and Giroux, New York, h/b, 1994.
In the Twilight Slot, Enitharmon, London, London, p/b, 1995.
Jamesian (broadside), New York Transit Authority in Cooperation with the Poetry Society of America, New York, 1995.
Dancing David, Nadja, Kripplebush, New York, h/b + p/b, 1996.
Jack Straw's Castle, Faber, (The Faber Library), London, 1997.
Frontiers of Gossip, Robert L. Barth, Edgewood, Kentucky, p/b,1998.
The Dump (broadside), Dia Center for the Arts, New York, 1998.

June (broadside), Wood Works, Seattle Washington, 1998.
Boss Cupid, Faber, London, h/b, 2000.

Editions

Poetry from Cambridge, 1951-52, The Fortune Press, London, h/b, 1952.
Five American Poets: Edgar Bowers, Howard Nemerov, Hyam Plutzik, Louis Simpson, William Stafford (with Ted Hughes), Faber, London, h/b, 1963.
Selected Poems of Fulke Greville, Faber, London, h/b, 1968 / University of Chicago Press, Illinois, h/b, 1969.
Ben Jonson, Penguin Books, Middlesex, p/b, 1974.
Poems by Charlie Hinkle (with William McPherson), Thom Gunn and William McPherson, San Francisco, California, p/b, 1988.

Uncollected Poems

'Hide and Seek', *Delta*, 1, Cambridge, Autumn, 1953, p. [8].
'Words in Action', *Spectator*, 192:6559, London, March 12, 1954, p. 288.
'Terms', *Spectator*, 192:6562, London, April 2, 1954, p. 398.
'Hungry', *London Magazine*, 1:4, London, May, 1954, p. 26.
'Palinode', *London Magazine*, 1:4, London, May, 1954, pp. 25-26.
'Ralph's Dream', *London Magazine*, 2:1, London, January, 1955, pp. 48-51.
'A District in Rome', *London Magazine*, 2:7, London, July, 1955, p. 14.
'The Paraplegic Lying on his Back', *London Magazine*, 2:7, London, July, 1955, pp. 13-14.
'An Inhabitant', *London Magazine*, 7:5, London, May, 1960, pp. 14-15.
'Signs of an Undertaking', *Spectator*, 205:6899, London, September 16, 1960, p. 409.
'A School of Resistance', *Paris Review*, 25, New York, Winter-Spring, 1961, p. 52.
'Telegraph Avenue', *Encounter*, 16:3, London, March, 1961, p. 3.
'Kurfürstendamm', *Observer*, London, September 24, 1961, p. 28.
'Out of Breath', *Encounter*, 18:1, London, January, 1962, p. 96.
'Third Avenue', *Observer*, London, July 28, 1963, p. 21.
'The Doctor's Own Body', *Observer*, London, December 15, 1963, p. 25.
'The Dying Lady', *Observer*, London, February 9, 1964, p. 26.
'Tending Bar', *Critical Quarterly*, 6:1, Spring, 1964, pp. 33-34.
'The Old Man in the Britannia', *Poetry*, 109:2, Chicago, Illinois, November, 1966, p. 70.
'Fillmore Auditorium', *Occident*, 1, Berkeley, California, Spring-Summer, 1967, pp. 60-61.
'North Kent', *Listener*, 79:2030, London, February 22, 1968, p. 231.
'The Naked Peace Marchers', *Journal for the Protection of All Beings*, 3 (Green Flag Issue), San Francisco, California, 1969, p. [29].
'The Stream', *Blackfish*, 3, Burnaby, BC, Canada, Summer, 1972, p. [20].
'Setting Out', *Listener*, 90:2311, London, July 12, 1973, p. 48.
'Walker', *Christopher Street*, 2:4, New York, October, 1977, p. 50.
'3AM', *London Magazine*, 17:6, London, December, 1977, pp. 15-16.
'The Sad Satanist', *Berkeley Review*, 6-7, Berkeley, California, Spring, 1978, p. 109.
'Holiday', *New Poetry*, 26:4, Sydney, December, 1978-February, 1979, p. 48.
'The Parrot House', *American Poetry Review*, 8:6, Philadelphia, Pennsylvania, November-December, 1979, p. 46.
'The VD Clinic', *American Poetry Review*, 8:6, Philadelphia, Pennsylvania, November-De-

cember, 1979, p. 46.
'Buchanan Castle, 1948', *London Magazine*, 19:9-10, London, December, 1979-January, 1980, p. 45.
'Wedding', *Christopher Street*, 4:9, New York, May, 1980, p. 29.
'The Married Men', *PN Review*, 24, 8:4, Manchester, November, 1981, p. 21.
'The Inside-Outside Game', *Massachusetts Review*, 23:1, Amherst, Massachusetts, Spring, 1982, p. 129.
'The Libertine', *Massachusetts Review*, 23:1, Amherst, Massachusetts, Spring, 1982, p. 129.
'The Wart', *Massachusetts Review*, 23:1, Amherst, Massachusetts, Spring, 1982, p. 130.
'Hell's Angel Listening to Jefferson Airplane', *Massachusetts Review*, 23:1, Amherst, Massachusetts, Spring, 1982, p. 131.
'Nice Thing', *Massachusetts Review*, 23:1, Amherst, Massachusetts, Spring, 1982, p. 132.
'Silence', *Massachusetts Review*, 23:1, Amherst, Massachusetts, Spring, 1982, p. 133.
'The Stylist', *A Just God*, 1:1, New York, November, 1982, p. 91.
'Visionary Firefighters', *PN Review*, 40, 11:2, Manchester, June, 1984, p. 14.
'Disco Kidnap', *New Sins*, 2, Chicago, Illinois, February, 1986, p. [2].
'Song of the Garden', *Galley Sail Review*, 25, 7:2, Berkeley, California, Summer, 1986, p. 3.
'The Liberty Granted', *In Folio*, 29, Cambridge, August 8, 1986, pp. [2-3].
'Is it Really True', *Galley Sail Review*, 32, 9:3, Berkeley, California, Winter, 1988-1989, p. A1.
'The Man in the Helmet', *Ploughshares*, 15:4, Boston, Massachusetts, Winter, 1890-1990, pp. 94-95.
'The Deeper', *Threepenny Review*, 43, 11:3, Berkeley, California, Autumn, 1990, October 5-11, 1990.
'Post Script: The Panel', *Threepenny Review*, 50, 13:2, Berkeley, California, Summer, 1992, p. 35.
'Herculaneum', *Conjunctions*, 19, Annandale-on-Hudson, New York, November, 1992, pp. 139-141.
'Clean Clothes', *Occident*, Berkeley, California, 1995.
'This Morning Light', in *The Blind See Only This World: Poems for John Wieners*, Granary Books, Boston, Massachusetts, 2000.

Uncollected Essays, Forewords, Introductions, Profiles, Reviews

(Essay) '"Oasis": an Experiment in Selling Poetry', *Bookseller*, 2412, London, March 15, 1952, pp. 782-785.
(Review of) F.R. Leavis, *The Common Pursuit*, *Cambridge Today*, 5:18, Cambridge, Lent Term, 1952, p. 14.
(Review of) Paul Dehn, *Romantic Landscape*, *Granta*, 56:1136, Cambridge, November 1, 1952, p.26.
(Profile) 'Tony White', *Varsity*, 17:5, Cambridge, November 8, 1952, p. 4.
(Review of) J.A. Hunter, *Hunter*, *Granta*, 56:1141, Cambridge, March 7, 1953, p. 23.
(Review of) G.S. Fraser and Ian Fletcher, eds., *Springtime*, *Gadfly*, 2:2, May 30, 1953, p. 27.
(Review of) Robert Graves, *Poems 1953*, *Gadfly*, 3:3, October 31, 1953, pp. 35-36.
(Review of) Muriel Spark, John Masefield, *New Statesman and Nation*, 46:1185, London, November 21, 1953, p. 651.
(Review of) Robert Penn Warren, *Brother to Dragons: a Tale in Verse and Voices*, *Spectator*, 192:6574, London, June 25, 1954, p. 795.
(Essay), 'Letter from Cambridge', *London Magazine*, 1:7, August, 1954, pp. 66-69.

(Review of) Frederick C. Gill, *The Romantic Movement and Methodism*, *Spectator*, 193:6581, London, August 13, 1954, p. 211.

(Review of) Christopher Isherwood, *The World in the Evening*, *London Magazine*, 1:9, October, 1954, pp. 81-85.

(Review of) William Empson, *Collected Poems*, *London Magazine*, 3:2, London, February, 1956, pp. 70-75.

(Review of) Wallace Stevens, *Collected Poems*, *London Magazine*, 3:4, London, April, 1956, pp. 81-84.

(Introduction and Notes to) *Young American Poets 1956*, *London Magazine*, 3:8, London, August, 1956, pp. 21-22, 34-35.

(Review of) Edgar Bowers, *The Form of Loss*, Donald F. Drummond, *The Battlement*, Thomas Cole, *A World of Saints*, Stephen Stepanchev, *Three Priests in April*, Lee Anderson, *Poets of Today, III: The Floating World and Other Poems*, Spencer Brown, *My Father's Business and Other Poems*; Joseph Langland, *The Green Town*, Katherine Hoskins, *Villa Narcisse*, *Poetry*, 89:4, Chicago, Illinois, January, 1957.

(Essay) 'Thom Gunn Writes ...', *Poetry Book Society Bulletin*, 14, London, May, 1957, pp. 1-2.

(Review of) James Reeves, *The Modern Poet's World*, W.G. Bebbington, *Introducing Modern Poetry*, *Spectator*, 199:6735, London, July 26, 1957, pp. 140, 142.

(Review of) George Barker, *Collected Poems, 1930-1955*, *Spectator*, 199:6736, London, August 2, 1957, p. 167.

(Review of) Louise Bogan, *Collected Poems*, *Spectator*, 199:6739, London, August 23, 1957, p. 254.

(Review of) John Bayley, *The Romantic Survival: a Study in Poetic Evolution*, *London Magazine*, 4:9, London, September, 1957, pp. 76-79.

(Review of) Robert Graves, *Robert Graves: Poems Selected by Himself*, *Spectator*, 199:6741, London, September 6, 1957, p. 311.

(Review of) Robert Langbaum, *The Poetry of Experience*, Frank Kermode, *Romantic Image*, *London Magazine*, 5:2, London, February, 1958, pp. 62-65.

(Review of) Geoffrey Moore, *Poetry Today*, *Spectator*, 200:6778, London, May 23, 1958, p. 661.

(Review of) John Heath-Stubbs, *The Triumph of the Muse and Other Poems*, John Hollander, *A Crackling of Thorns*, Jon Silkin, *The Two Freedoms*, *Spectator*, 201:6789, London, August 8, 1958, p. 200.

(Review of) Roy Fuller, *Brutus's Orchard*, William Meredith, *The Open Sea and Other Poems*, Anthony Thwaite, *Home Truths*, Pauline Hanson, *The Forever Young and Other Poems*, *Poetry*, 92:6, Chicago, Illinois, September, 1958, pp. 378-384.

(Review of) Anthony Cronin, *Poems*, Gordon Wharton, *Errors of Observation*, Donald Davie, *A Winter Talent and Other Poems*, *Listen*, 3:1, Hessle, Yorkshire, Winter, 1958, pp. 12-14, 19-22.

(Review of) W.C. Williams, *Paterson* (Book Five), E.E. Cummings, *95 Poems*, Muriel Rukeyser, *Body of Waking*, Jose Garcia Villa, *Selected Poems and New*, Karl Shapiro, *Poems of a Jew*, John Ciardi, *A Sheaf of Love Poems*, David Wagoner, *A Place to Stand*, Donald Hall, *The Dark Houses*, Alan Stephens, *The Sum*, *Yale Review*, 48:2, New Haven, Connecticut, December, 1958, pp. 297-305.

(Review of) Kenneth Rexroth, *In Defense of the Earth*, Thomas Blackburn, *The Next Word*, C.A. Trypanis, *The Cocks of Hades*, Christopher Logue, *The Man Who Told His Love*, *Spectator*, 202:6816, London, February 13, 1959, pp. 234-235.

(Review of) Donald Hall, Robert Pack and Louis Simpson, eds., *The New Poets of England and America*, Louis Simpson, *Good News of Death*, Edgar Bowers, *The Form of Loss*, *Spectator*, 202:6822, London, March 27, 1959, p. 443.

(Review of) Dan Jacobson, *No Further West: California Visited, Spectator,* 202:6831, London, May 29, 1959, p. 783.
(Review of) Charles Tomlinson, *Seeing is Believing,* Donald Hall, *The Dark Houses,* Howard Nemerov, *Mirrors and Windows: Poems, American Scholar,* 28:3, Washington DC, Summer, 1959, pp. 390, 392, 394, 396.
(Review of) Earl of Birkenhead, ed., *John Betjeman's Collected Poems,* Alastair Reid, *Oddments, Inklings, Omens, Moments: Poems,* Elizabeth Jennings, *A Sense of the World,* Louis O. Coxe, *The Wilderness and Other Poems,* Barbara Gibbs, *The Green Chapel,* Ned O'Gorman, *The Night of the Hammer,* Theodore Roethke, *Words for the Wind, Yale Review,* 48:4, New Haven, Connecticut, June, 1959, pp. 617-626.
(Review of) G.S. Fraser, *Vision and Rhetoric: Studies in Modern Poetry,* John Press, *The Chequer'd Shade: Reflections on Obscurity in Poetry, London Magazine,* 6:10, London, October, 1959, pp. 61-64.
(Review of) Delmore Schwarz, *Summer Knowledge,* James Wright, *Saint Judas,* Louis Simpson, *A Dream of Governors,* Barbara Howes, *Light and Dark,* Hyam Plutzik, *Apples from Shinar,* Reed Whittemore, *The Self-Made Man,* Hayden Carruth, *The Crow and the Heart,* William Dickey, *Of the Festivity,* Robert Lowell, *Life Studies, Yale Review,* 49:2, New Haven, Connecticut, December, 1959, pp. 295-305.
(Essay) 'Disciplined Richness', *Poetry Northwest,* 1:3, Seattle, Washington, Winter, 1960, p. 19.
(Review of) Ezra Pound, *Thrones, 96-109 De Los Cantares,* George Starbuck, *Bone Thoughts,* Kenneth Koch, *Ko, or a Season on Earth,* Jean Garrigue, *A Water Walk by Villa d'Este,* Carol Hall, *Portrait of Your Niece,* Ruth Stone, *In an Iridescent Time,* Donald Justice, *The Summer Anniversaries, Yale Review,* 49:4, New Haven, Connecticut, June, 1960, pp. 589-598.
(Review of) J.V. Cunningham, *The Exclusions of a Rhyme,* Lawrence Durrell, *Collected Poems,* Harold Moss, *A Winter Come, a Summer Gone,* Louis Grudin, *An Eye in the Sky,* W.H. Auden, *Homage to Clio, Yale Review,* 50:1, New Haven, Connecticut, September, 1960, pp. 125-135.
(Review of) Yvor Winters, *In Defense of Reason, London Magazine,* 7:10, London, October, 1960, pp. 64-66.
(Review of) J.C. Squire, *Collected Poems,* James Kirkup, *The Prodigal Son,* William Plomer, *Collected Poems,* Vernon Watkins, *Ballad of the Marie Lwyd* and *Cypress and Acacia,* Donald Davie, *The Forests of Lithuania,* Ted Hughes, *Lupercal, Poetry,* 97:4, Chicago, Illinois, January, 1961, pp. 260-270.
(Review of) Howard Nemerov, *New and Selected Poems,* W.S. Merwin, *The Drunk in the Furnace,* Hyam Plutzik, *Horatio,* Ralph Pomeroy, *Stills and Movies,* David Ignatow, *Say Pardon,* Charles Olson, *The Distances, Yale Review,* 50:4, New Haven, Connecticut, June, 1961, pp. 585-596.
(Review of) Robert Lowell, *Imitations,* Richard Wilbur, *Advice to a Prophet,* Louis MacNeice, *Solstices,* Maxine Kumin, *Halfway,* William Stafford, *West of Your City,* Thomas Kinsella, *Poems and Translations,* Ruthven Todd, *Garland for the Winter Solstice, Yale Review,* 51:3, New Haven, Connecticut, March, 1962, pp. 480-489.
(Review of) Robert Conquest, *Between Mars and Venus, Spectator,* 208:6984, London, May 4, 1962, p. 596.
(Review of) Denise Levertov, *The Jacob's Ladder,* Robert Creeley, *For Love (Poems, 1950-1960),* James Dickey, *Drowning with Others,* Robert Watson, *A Paper Horse,* Horace Gregory, *Medusa in Gramercy Park,* Robert Conquest, *Between Mars and Venus,* John Hollander, *Movie-Going and Other Poems,* Donald Davie, *New and Selected Poems, Yale Review,* 52:1, New Haven, Connecticut, pp. 129-138.
(Essay) 'In Nobody's Pantheon', *Shenandoah,* 13:2, Lexington, Virginia, Winter, 1962, pp.

[34]-35.
(Review of) Christopher Middleton, *Torse 3,* Adrienne Rich, *Poems, 1954-1962,* Charles Gullans, *Arrivals and Departures,* Anne Sexton, *All My Pretty Ones,* Weldon Kees, *Collected Poems,* Robert Bly, *Silence in the Snowy Fields, Yale Review,* 53:1, New Haven, Connecticut, October, 1963, pp. 135-144.
(Essay) 'What Hope for Poetry?', *Granta,* 68:1229, Cambridge, October 19, 1963, p. 8.
(Review of) Alan Stephens, *Between Matter and Principle,* Philip Levine, *On the Edge,* Louis MacNeice, *The Burning Perch,* James Wright, *The Branch Will Not Break,* Louis Simpson, *At the End of the Open Road, Yale Review,* 53:3, New Haven, Connecticut, March, 1964, pp. 447-458.
(Essay) 'Poets in Control', *Twentieth Century,* 173:1024, London, Winter, 1964-1965, pp. 102-106.
(Essay) 'The New Music', *Listener,* 78:2001, London, August 3, 1967, pp. [129]-130.
(Essay) 'Thom Gunn Writes ...', *Poetry Book Society Bulletin,* 54, London, September, 1967, p. 1.
(Review of) Gary Snyder, *The Back Country* and *Six Sections from Mountains and Rivers without End, Listener,* 79:2040, London, May 2, 1968, pp. 576-577.
(Review of) Rod Taylor, *Florida East Coast Champion, Poetry,* 121:4, Chicago, Illinois, January, 1973, pp. 239-241.
(Review of) Donald Davie, *Thomas Hardy and British Poetry* and *Collected Poems, 1950-1970, New York Times Book Review,* New York, January 7, 1973, pp. 5, 26.
(Review of) Dick Davies, *In the Distance, Thames Poetry,* 1:2, London, Summer, 1976, pp. 59-62.
(Essay) 'Thom Gunn Writes ...', *Poetry Book Society Bulletin,* 90, London, Autumn, 1976, p. [1].
(Essay) 'The Openness of Donald Davie', *Sequoia,* 22:2, Stanford, California, Winter, 1977, pp. 30-32.
(Review of) James Purdy, *Dream Palaces, Threepenny Review,* 3, 1:3, Berkeley, California, Autumn, 1980, p. 7.
(Review of) W.S. Graham, *Selected Poems,* Alfred Corn, *The Various Light,* Aaron Shurin, *Giving Up the Ghost,* Timothy Steele, *Uncertainties and Rest, Threepenny Review,* 6, 2:2, Berkeley, California, Summer, 1981, pp. 4-5.
(Review of) Raymond Oliver, *Entries, Occident,* 101:1, Berkeley, California, Autumn, 1981, pp. 47-48.
(Review of) Basil Bunting, *Collected Poems,* Carroll F. Terrell, ed., *Basil Bunting: Man and Poet, Threepenny Review,* 10, 3:2, Berkeley, California, Summer, 1982, pp. 6-7.
(Essay) 'Thom Gunn Writes ...', P*oetry Book Society Bulletin,* 113, London, Summer, 1982, pp. [1-2].
(Essay) 'Pushy Jews and Aging Queens: Imaginary People in Two Novels by Coleman Dowell', *Review of Contemporary Fiction,* 2:3, Elmwood Park, Illinois, Autumn, 1982, pp. 135-145.
(Essay) Untitled obituary for Josephine Miles, *California Monthly,* 95:6, Berkeley, California, June-July, 1985, p. 29.
(Essay) 'A Poet's Critic', *PN Review,* 48, 12:4, Manchester, December, 1985, p. 59.
(Review of) Patricia Willis, ed., *Marianne Moore: the Complete Prose,* Taffy Martin, *Marianne Moore,* John M. Slatin, *The Savage's Romance, Times Literary Supplement,* 4375, London, February 6, 1987, pp. 127-128.
(Review) of Thomas Parkinson, *Poets, Poems, Movements, San Francisco Chronicle Review,* San Francisco, California, August 16, 1987, p. 9.
(Essay) Untitled Essay about Mina Loy, *Poetry Pilot,* New York, November, 1987, pp. 6-7.
(Review of) A. Walton Litz and Christopher MacGowan, eds., *William Carlos Williams, The*

Collected Poems, Volume 1, *Times Literary Supplement*, 4429, London, February 19, 1988, pp. 179-180.

(Review of) Edward Mendelson, ed., *Plays by W.H. Auden and Christopher Isherwood: and other Dramatic Writings* and *Writings by W.H. Auden, 1928-1938*, Los Angeles Times Book Review, Los Angeles, California, January 29, 1989, p. 2.

(Essay) 'Robert Duncan's Romantic Modernism', *European Gay Review*, 4, London, Spring, 1989, pp. 54-55.

(Review of) Harold Brodkey, *Stories in an Almost Classical Mode*, *Threepenny Review*, 37, 10:1, Berkeley, California, Spring, 1989, p. 12.

(Review of) *Presences of Mind: the Collected Books of Jack Sharpless*, *Bay Area Reporter*, 20:10, San Francisco, California, March 8, 1990, p. 31.

(Review of) Peter Dale Scott, *Coming of Age in Jakarta*, *Times Literary Supplement*, 4583, London, February 1, 1991, p. 19.

(Introduction to) Anne Winters, *A Poet's Sampler*, *Boston Review*, 16:3-4, Boston, Massachusetts, June-August, 1991, p. 26.

(Essay), 'Two Saturday Nights', *Sine Over Tan*, 1, Toronto, August 26, 1991, pp. 2, 4-5.

(Essay) Contribution on Darwin's *Voyage of the Beagle* to 'International Books of the Year: a Further Selection from Sixteen Writers', *Times Literary Supplement*, 4628, London, December 13, 1991, pp. 12-13.

(Essay/Review of) Luc Santé, *Low Life*, *Threepenny Review*, 48, 12:4, Berkeley, California, Winter, 1992, pp. 3-4.

(Essay) 'Thom Gunn Writes on his New Collection', *Poetry Book Society Bulletin*, 152, London, Spring, 1992, p. 5.

(Essay) Contribution on Clive Wilmer's *Of Earthly Paradise* to 'International Books of the Year: Thirty-Four Writers Select the Books that Most Impressed Them in 1992', *Times Literary Supplement*, 4679, London, December 4, 1992, pp. 9-13.

(Essay) 'A Heroic Enterprise', in Robert Polito, ed., *A Reader's Guide to The Changing Light at Sandover*, University of Michigan Press, Ann Arbor, Michigan, 1994, pp. 153-157.

(Essay) 'Boyd's Sonnet', *PN Review*, 19:2, Manchester, 1992, pp. 26-27.

(Review of) Eliot Weinburger, ed., *American Poetry Since 1950: Innovations and Outsiders*, *PN Review*, 20:6, Manchester, 1994, pp. 22-26.

(Essay) 'Leper of the Moon: Mina Loy's Tough Epiphanies of the Streets', *Times Literary Supplement*, 4874, London, August 30, 1996, pp. 3-4.

(Essay) 'Starting to Read Ark', *Chicago Review*, 42:1, Chicago, Illinois, 1996, pp. 21-22.

(Foreword to) Bob Cant, ed., *Invented Identities?*, Cassell, London, 1997.

(Review of) Richard Caddel and Anthony Flowers, *Basil Bunting – a Northern Life*, *Times Literary Supplement*, 4943, London, December 26, 1997, p. 24.

(Essay) 'Syllabics', Appendix to Jon Silkin, *The Life of Metrical and Free Verse in the Twentieth Century*, Macmillan, London, h/b + p/b, 1997/ St Martin's Press, New York, h/b, 1997, pp. 374-376.

TRANSLATIONS

CHINESE

The Neighbor's Flute, ed. Lu Yüan, with a translation by Lu Yüan of 'Breakfast', People's Literature Publishing House, Beijing, 1987, pp. 184-186.

Czech

Smylsl Pohybu, with translations by Jiri Konupek of five poems by TG, *Sveetova literatura*, 4, Prague, 1958, 107-111.

Dutch

Wij Twee Jongens: Mannelijke Homoseksualiteit in de Zoste-eeuwse Literatuur, een Internationale Bloemlezing, eds. David Galloway and Christian Sabisch, with translations by Tjark Keijzer, Adriaan Vreugdenhil, and Gerard Verbart of four poems by TG, Manteau, Amsterdam, 1984, pp. 264-268.

Spiegel van de Engelse Poëzie uit de Gehele Wereld: Dichters van de Twintigste Eeuw, eds. Elizabeth Mollison and Henk Romijn Meijer, with translations of three poems by TG, Meulenhoff Nederland bv, Amsterdam, 1989.

German

Gedichte Philip Larkin, Thom Gunn, Ted Hughes, ed. Karl-Heinz Berger, with translations by Helmut Heinrich, Klaus-Dieter Sommer and Karl-Heinz Berger of nineteen poems by TG, Verlag Volk und Welt, Berlin, 1974.

Heiligenlob Moderner Dichter, ed. Gisbert Kranz, with a translation by Gisbert Kranz of one poem by TG, Verlag Friedrich Pustet, Regensburg, 1975.

Moderne Englische Lyrik, ed. Willi Erzgräber, with translations by Ute and Werner Knoedgen of six poems by TG, Philipp Reclam Jun, Stuttgart, 1976.

Calamus: Männliche Homosexualität in der Literatur des 20. Jahrhunderts: Eine Anthologie, eds. David Galloway and Christian Sabisch, with translations by Uwe Herms of three poems by TG, Rowalt Verlag Gmbh, Reinbek bei Hamburg, 1981, pp. 343-[347].

Welches Tier Gehort Zu Dir? Eine Poetische Arche Noah, ed. Peter Hamm, with a translation by Peter Hamm of 'Considering the Snail', Carl Hanser Verlag, Munich, 1984, pp. 302-303.

'Considering the Snail', translation by Ursula Spinner, *Neue Zürcher Zeitung*, 2909: 75, Zurich, July 5, 1964, p.4.

Ensemble 4 Lyrik Prosa Essay, with translations by Helmut Winter of three poems by TG, *Internationales Jahrbuch für Literatur*, Langen Müller, Munich, March 27, 1973.

Italian

I Miei Tristi Capitani e Altre Poesie, translation by Camillo Pennati of *My Sad Captains and Other Poems*, with a preface by Agostino Lombardo, Arnoldo Mondadori Editori, Milan, 1968.

Tatto, translation by Luciano Erba of *Touch*, with an introduction by Nemi D'Agostino, Ugo Guanda, Milan, 1979.

Poesia Inglese del Dopoguerra, ed. Robert Sanesi, with translations by Roberto Sanesi of five poems by TG, Schwartz Editore, Milan, 1958.

Poesia Inglese del '900 (third edition only), introduced and with notes by Carlo Izzo, with translations by Carlo Izzo of five poems by TG, Ugo Guanda, Parma, 1967.

'"Riti di Passagio" e Altri Versi', translations by Camillo Pennati of 'Rites of Passage' and ten other poems by TG), *Almanaco dello specchio*, Milan, February 3, 1974, 148-175.

Japanese

Fighting Terms (translation of the Faber p/b issue of *Fighting Terms*), Etude Group, Etude Group, Kyoto, 1977.
Gendai Shishu, ed. Hajime Shinoda, with translations by Satoshi Nakagawa of seven poems by TG, Shueisha Publishing Co., Ltd., Tokyo, 1968.

Portuguese

Talbot Road, translation by Antonio Feijo, *As Escadas não têm Degraus*, Lisbon, March 3, 1990, pp. 90-101.

Spanish

Poesia Ingelesa Contemporanea, edited, and with an introduction and notes by E.L. Revol, with translations by E.L. Revol of two poems by TG, Ediciones Librerias Fausto, Buenos Aires, 1974.
Artics, 8, with translations by Joan Ferranté of three poems by TG, September-November, 1987, pp. 23-26.

Swedish

Atta Engelska Poeter, eds. Petter Bergman and Göran Printz-Pahlson (with translations by Göran Printz-Pahlson of three poems by TG), Lyrikklub, Stockholm, 1957.
USA Poesi 700 dikter fran 1010-1983, ed. Jan Verner-Carlsson, with translation by Lars Gustav Hellström of the one line TG contributed to 'The Great American Poem', a 'round-robin' poem compiled by Philip Dacey and published in *Antaeus*, 32, Winter 1979, line 64, p. 84, Förlaget Café Existens, 1984.

Musical Settings

The Cat and the Wind, for Soprano and Piano, music composed by Allan Blank, American Composers Alliance, New York, 1979.
Back to Life, for Counter-Tenor and Double Bass, music composed by Ned Rorem, Boosey and Hawkes, 1980.

Interviews

Michael Kitay, Julian Jebb, Ronald Hayman, 'Interview', *Chequer*, 6, Summer, 1954, pp. 17-19.
Ian Hamilton, 'Four Conversations', *London Magazine*, 4:6, November, 1964, pp. 64-70.
'Love Me, Love My Poem', *Observer*, March 7, 1965, p. 23.
Hilary Morrish, 'Violence and Energy: an Interview', *Poetry Review*, 57:1, Spring, 1966, pp. 32-35.
Claudia Collins, Patrick Condon, Frank Schaller, Robert Vianello, Bruce White, 'An Interview with Thom Gunn', *Cauldron*, Winter, 1969, Kalamazoo College, MI, pp.12-17.
'Thom Gunn', in *The Unstrung Lyre: Interviews with Fourteen Poets*, ed. Henri Coulette, National Endowment for the Arts, Washington, DC, 1971.

Hank Newer, 'Interview with Thom Gunn', *Brushfire*, 25, 1975-76, Reno, Nevada, pp. 155-159.
Pico Iyer, 'Thom Gunn and the Pacific Drift', *Isis*, June 2, 1977, Oxford, pp. 20-21.
Tony Sarver, 'Thom Gunn', *Advocate*, 220, July 27, 1977, San Mateo, California, pp. 39-40.
W.I. Scobie, 'Gunn in America: a Conversation in San Francisco', *London Magazine*, 17:6, December 1977, pp. [5]-15.
'The Books in My Life: Gay Writers, Critics and Teachers Select Their Favorite Books', *Sentinel*, 5:25, December 15, 1978, San Francisco, California, p.9.
Nicholas de Jongh, 'Nicholas de Jongh Meets the Emigré Poet Thom Gunn on the Circuit Again: the Changing Face of the Brando Bard', *Guardian*, London, November 14, 1979, p. 9.
Steve Abbott, 'Poet Thom Gunn on Keats, Cruising and Other Matters', *Sentinel*, 7:11, May 30, 1980, San Francisco, California, p. 26.
John Haffenden, *Viewpoints: Poets in Conversation with John Haffenden*, Faber, London, 1981, pp. 35-56.
Alan Hiller, 'Writing in Style: an Interview with Thom Gunn', *Amherst Student*, 110:45, April 30, 1981, Amherst College, Massachusetts, p.4.
Helen Deutsch and Ted Braun, 'Voice of the Poet', *In Other Words*, 2:7, May 8, 1981, Amherst College, Massachusetts, pp. 8-9, 11.
Kavita Malhotra, 'Gunn's poetry is debate between passions', *News Record*, 69:9, October 30, 1981, University of Cincinnati, Ohio, p. 3.
Steve Abbott, 'Writing One's Own [*Sic:* Own] Mythology: an Interview with Thom Gunn', *Contact II*, 5:26, Summer, 1982, New York, pp. 20-24.
Jhan Hochman, 'An interview with Thom Gunn', *Portland Review*, 2:1, Autumn, 1982, Portland, Oregon, pp. 71-78.
Mickey Friedman, 'A Poet More Famous Abroad Than at Home', *San Francisco Examiner*, September 6, 1982, California, p. B3.
Joe Shakarchi, 'The Thom Gunn interview', *Poetry Flash*, 117, December 1982, Berkeley, California, pp. 2, 10.
Eds. John Banta and Alex Stoll, 'Conversations with Thom Gunn', *Leviathan*, 10:2, January, 1984, Colorado College, Colorado Springs, Colorado, pp. 7-8.
Hank Nuwer, 'Thom Gunn: Britain's Expatriate Poet', *Rendezvous,* 21:1, Autumn, 1985, Idaho State University, Pocatello, Idaho, pp. 68-78 / reprinted in Hank Nuwer, *Rendezvousing with Contemporary Writers*, Idaho State University Press, Pocatello, Idaho, 1988, pp. 68-78.
Graham Fawcett, 'Thom Gunn's Castle', transcript of interview recorded by the BBC, London, recorded June 3, 1985, broadcast Radio 3, March 4, 1986.
Lee Bartlett, *Talking Poetry: Conversations in the Workshop with Contemporary Poets*, University of New Mexico Press, Albuquerque, New Mexico, 1987, pp. 88-101.
August Kleinzahler and John Tranter, 'An interview with Thom Gunn', *Scripsi*, 5:3, April, 1989, Parkville, Australia, pp. 173-194.
Alan Sinfield, 'Thom Gunn at Sixty', *Gay Times*, 131, London, August, 1989, pp. 26-29 / reprinted as 'Thom Gunn in San Francisco' in *Critical Survey*, 2:2, 1990, Oxford, pp. [223]-230.
Marc Breindel, 'Thom Gunn: SF Poet Thom Gunn Cruises and Trips through the 20th Century', *San Francisco Sentinel*, 16:32, August 5, 1988, San Francisco, California, pp. 19, 22-23.
Jim Powell, 'An interview with Thom Gunn', *PN Review*, 70, 16:2, Autumn, 1989, Manchester, pp. 52-56 / reprinted in Thom Gunn, *Shelf-Life* [see BOOKS, BROADSIDES AND PAMPHLETS above].
Jean W. Ross, in ed. James G. Lesniak, *Contemporary Authors: New Revision Series Volume*

33, Gale Research Inc., Detroit, MI, 1991, pp. 197-199.
Alan Jenkins, 'In Time of Plague' (an interview and a review of *The Man with Night Sweats*), *Independent on Sunday*, February 1, 1992, London, pp. 24-25.
Elgy Gillespie, 'Poems of the Plague' (an interview and a review of *The Man with Night Sweats*)*Guardian*, February 24, 1992, London, p. 33 .
Steven Saylor, 'Thom Gunn on Love in the Time of AIDS', *San Francisco Review of Books*, 16:4, March 1992, San Francisco, California, pp. 14-16.
David Gewanter, 'An Interview with Thom Gunn', *Agni*, 36, October, 1992, Boston, Massachusetts, pp. 289-299.
Lisa K. Buchanan, 'Smoking Gunn: Poet Thom Gunn Tackles AIDS with Uncommon Lyricism', *San Francisco Focus*, 39:11, November, 1992, San Francisco, California, p. 32.
Lee Jago, 'Thom Gunn (1942-47): The Laundromat Cowboy', *Gower*, 52:3, December, 1992, University College School, London, pp. 16-18.
Kate Kellaway, 'A Poet Who's Still Firing on all Cylinders', *Observer*, December 13, 1992, London, p. 48.
Billy Lux, 'An Interview with Thom Gunn', *Channel* 34, New York, Videoland, 1995.
Clive Wilmer, 'Thom Gunn: the Art of Poetry', LXXII, *Paris Review*, 135, New York, Summer, 1995, pp. [142]-189.
Stefania Michelucci, 'Cole Street, San Francisco: a Conversation with Thom Gunn', *Quaderni del Dipartimento di Lingue e Letteratura Straniere Moderne*, 8, University of Genoa, 1996, pp. 261-288.

RECORDINGS

DISCS AND AUDIOCASSETTES

Listen Presents Thom Gunn Reading 'On the Move' [and other poems], one disc, The Marvell Press, Hessle, Yorkshire, 1962, LPV4.
The Jupiter Anthology of 20th Century English Poetry, Part III, ed. Anthony Thwaite, 1 disc, Jupiter Recordings, London, 1963, JUR 00A8.
Anthology of 20th Century English Poetry, Part III, ed. Anthony Thwaite, 1 disc, A Jupiter Recording issued by Folkways, Folkways Records & Service Corporation, New York, 1967, Florida 9879.
The Jupiter Anthology, Part Three 00A8, ed. Anthony Thwaite, 1 audiocassette, Audio-Visual Productions, London, 1975.
The Poet Speaks, Record 5: Ted Hughes, Peter Porter, Thom Gunn, Sylvia Plath, ed. Peter Orr, 1 disc, Argo Record Co., London, 1965.
Thom Gunn Reading His Own Poetry, 1 audiocassette, Audio-Visual Productions, London, 1971, 820/6.
British Poets of Our Time: Thom Gunn, ed. Peter Orr, 1 disc, Argo, The Decca Record Co., London, 1975, PLP 1203.
Thom Gunn Reading His Own Poetry, 1 audiocassette, The Library of Congress, Washington, DC, 233:T8186.
Thom Gunn and Craig Raine: A Faber Poetry Cassette, 1 audiocassette, Faber, London, 1983.

VIDEOCASSETTES

Thom Gunn Reading His Own Poetry, The American Poetry Archive, The Poetry Center, San Francisco University, California, 1974.

Thom Gunn, Nathaniel Tarn and Joanne Kyger Reading Their Own Poems, American Poetry Archive and Resource Center, The Videotape Collection of the Poetry Center at San Francisco State University, California, First Series, 1975, V-T 63/65.
Thom Gunn Introduces Ted Hughes, American Archive and Resource Center, The Videotape Collection of The Poetry Center at San Francisco State University, California, Third Series, 1978, V-T 218.
Thom Gunn Reading His Own Poetry, The American Poetry Archive, The Poetry Center, San Francisco University, California, 1986.
Thom Gunn Reading His Own Poetry, The American Poetry Archive, The Poetry Center, San Francisco University, California, 1990.
Thom Gunn Reading His Own Poetry, The Library of Congress, Washington, DC, 1991, LWO 27922; LWO 28275.
An Interview with Thom Gunn, Channel 34, New York, Videoland, New York, 1995.

Secondary Works

Critical Discussions

Abse, Dannie, ed. untitled, in *Corgi Modern Poets in Focus: 5*, Corgi Books, London, 1973, pp. 31-37.
Allott, Kenneth, ed. untitled, in *The Penguin Book of Contemporary Verse, 1918-60*, 2nd edition, Penguin Books, Middlesex, 1962, pp. 372-374.
Alpert, Barry, ed., untitled, in *Donald Davie: the Poet in the Imaginary Museum: Essays of Two Decades*, Carcanet, Manchester, 1977, pp. 75, 123, 182, 247-248.
Alvarez, A., 'Poetry of the Fifties in England', in John Wain, ed., *International Literary Journal*, 1, John Calder, London, 1958, pp. 97-107.
– 'English Poetry Today', in *Commentary*, 32:[3], New York, September 1961, pp. 217-223.
Anonymous, 'Poets of Moderation', *Times Literary Supplement*, 2837, London, July 13, 1956, p. 424.
Anonymous, 'Four Young Poets: IV, Thom Gunn', *Times Educational Supplement*, 2150, London, August 3, 1956, p. 995.
Anonymous, 'Poets of an Ousted Aristocracy', *Times Literary Supplement*, 3146, London, June 15, 1962, p. 447.
Arbasino, Alberto, *Sessanta Posizione*, Feltrinelli Editore, Milan, 1971, pp. 232-236 (in Italian).
Baskins, Dorothy A., *The Existentialist Hero in Thom Gunn's Poetry: 1954-1962*, MA thesis, University of Oregon, Eugene, Oregon, 1964.
Blackburn, Thomas, 'Poetry Today', in *English*, 18:100, London, Spring 1969, [12]-17.
Blaicher, Gunter, ed., *Deutschland in Britischer Dichtung seit 1945: eine Anthologie*, 11:5, Eichstäten Materialien, Regensburg, 1987, pp. 32, 55, 58 (in German).
Bloom, Harold, gen. ed., 'Thom Gunn', in *The Chelsea House Library of Literary Criticism: Twentieth Century British Literature*, 2 (E-H), Chelsea House Publishers, New York, 1986, pp. 999-1016.
Bold, Alan, ed., *Cambridge Book of English Verse, 1939-1975*, Cambridge University Press, Cambridge, 1976, pp. 222-228.
– *Gunn and Hughes*, Oliver and Boyd, Edinburgh, 1976.

Bolt, Sydney, 'Thom Gunn: Words in the Head', *Delta,* 43, Cambridge, June 1968, pp. [12]-16.
Brinnin, John Malcolm, and Bill Read, *The Modern Poets: an American-British Anthology,* McGraw-Hill Book Co., New York, 1963, p. 135.
Brown, Merle, 'Larkin and His Audience', *Iowa Review,* 8:4, Iowa, Autumn, 1977, pp. 117-134.
– 'The Authentic Duplicity of Thom Gunn's Recent Poetry', *Missouri Review,* 2:2-3, Columbia, Missouri, Spring, 1979, pp. 131-146.
– *Double Lyric: Divisiveness and Communal Creativity in Recent English Poetry,* Columbia University Press, 1980, pp. 1, 19, 76-77, 126-145, 178-200, 201, 202, 222.
Brownjohn, Alan, 'The Poetry of Thom Gunn', in *London Magazine,* 2:12, London, March 1963, [45]-52.
Campbell, James, 'The Leather-Clad Laureate', *Guardian,* London, May 1, 1999, p. 10.
– 'Thom Gunn, Anglo-American Poet', *Agenda,* 37:2-3, London, Autumn-Winter, 1999, pp. 70-74.
Carpenter, Peter, 'Thom Gunn's Bodies and the Poetry of Apprehension', *Agenda,* 37:2-3, London, Autumn-Winter, 1999, pp. 81-86.
Caserio, Robert L., 'The Mortal Limits of Poetry and Criticism: Reading Yingling, Reading Gunn', in Robyn Wiegman and Thomas E. Yingling, eds., *AIDS and the National Body,* Duke University Press, Durham, North Carolina, 1997.
Chainey, Graham, *A Literary History of Cambridge,* University of Michigan Press, Ann Arbor, Michigan, 1986, pp. 61, 217, 226, 227, 228-229, 230, 231, 236, 237.
Chambers, Douglas, 'The Poetic Implications of the Sensory Life', *PN Review,* 70, 16:2, Manchester, Autumn, 1989, pp. 31-32.
– 'Between That Disgust and This', *Agenda,* 37:2-3, London, Autumn-Winter, 1999, pp. 102-106.
Clunies-Ross, Pamela, 'Some Autobiographical Notes', in Richard Burns, ed., *Rivers of Life: a Gravesend Anthology,* The Victoria Press, Kent, 1980, pp. 105-107.
Conquest, Elizabeth Neece, *The Colour of Doubt: Movement Poetry,* PhD thesis, University of Southern California, Los Angeles, California, 1982, pp. 152-181.
Corcoran, Neil, 'Thom Gunn', in Thomas Riggs, ed., *Contemporary Poets,* 6th edition, St Martin's Press, New York, 1996, pp. 416-417.
Cox, C.B. and A.E. Dyson, *Modern Poetry: Studies in Practical Criticism,* Edward Arnold, London, 1963, pp. 147-152.
Cox, C.B. and A.E. Dyson, *The Practical Criticism of Poetry: a Text Book,* Edward Arnold, London, 1965, pp. 87-100.
– *Poems of this Century,* Edward Arnold, London, 1968, p. 134.
Culpepper, Thomas Allen, 'Homoerotic Poetics in Housman, Owen, Auden and Gunn', Postgraduate Thesis, University of Tulsa, 1998.
D'Agostino, Nemi, Introduction, in Thom Gunn, *Tatto,* Guanda, Milan, 1979, pp. 7-11 (in Italian).
Darlington, Andrew, 'Thom Gunn – a Sense of Movement', *Stable,* 3, Clare, Suffolk, January 1977, pp. 17-21.
Davie, Donald, 'Augustans New and Old', in *The Twentieth Century,* 158:945, London, November, 1955, pp. [464]-475.
– 'Thom Gunn', *PN Review,* 70, 16:2, Manchester, Autumn, 1989, p. 38.
Davies, Hugh Sykes, 'Cambridge Poetry', in *The Twentieth Century,* 157, London, January-June, 1955, pp. [149]-158.
Davis, Dick, *Wisdom and Wilderness: the Achievement of Yvor Winters,* University of Georgia Press, Athena, Georgia, 1983, pp. 103, 215.
– Untitled, *PN Review,* 70, 16:2, Manchester, Autumn, 1989, p. 32.

de Michelis, Lidia, *La Poesia di Thom Gunn*, La Nuova Italia Ditrice, Florence, 1978.
Dickey, James, 'In the Presence of Anthologies', *Sewanee Review*, 66:2, Tennessee, April-June, 1958, pp. [294]-314.
Dodsworth, Martin, 'Thom Gunn: Negatives and Positives', *the Review*, 18, London, April 1968, pp. 46-61.
- *The Survival of Poetry: a Contemporary Survey*, Faber, London, 1970, pp. 193-215.
- 'Gunn's Rhymes', *PN Review*, 70, 16:2, Manchester, Autumn, 1989, pp. 33-34.
- 'Gunn's Family of Man in "The Hug"', *Agenda*, 37:2-3, London, Autumn-Winter, 1999, pp. 75-80.
Dörfel, Hanspeter, 'Thom Gunn: "Breaking Ground"', in Elke Platz-Waury, ed., *Moderne Englische Lyrik: Interpretation und Dokumentation*, Quelle & Meyer, Heidelberg, 1978, pp. 186-205.
Dyson, A.E., *The Crazy Fabric: Essays in Irony*, Macmillan, London, 1965, p. 213.
- '"Watching you watching me ...", a Note on *The Passages of Joy*', in Dyson, A.E., ed., *Three Contemporary Poets: Thom Gunn, Ted Hughes and R.S. Thomas*, Macmillan, London, 1990, pp. 82-98.
Eagleton, Terry, 'Myth and History in Recent Poetry', in Michael Schmidt and Grevel Lindop, eds., *British Poetry Since 1960: A Critical Survey*, Carcanet, Oxford, 1972, pp. [233]-239.
Elon, Florence, 'The Movement Against Itself: British Poetry of the 1950s', *Southern Review*, 19:1, Baton Rouge, Louisiana, January, 1983, pp. 88-110.
Erzgraber, Willi, ed., *Moderne Englische Lyrik*, Philipp Reclam Jun., Stuttgart, 1976, pp. 515-518 (in German).
Esch, Arno, *Zur Situation der Zeitgenössischen Englischen Lyrik*, Westdeutscher Verlag, Opladen, 1980, pp. 17-24 (in German).
Faulkner, Peter, 'Matter and Spirit', *Agenda*, 37:2-3, London, Autumn-Winter, 1999, pp. 87-91.
Fawcett, Graham, 'Thom Gunn's Castle', transcript of interview recorded by the BBC, London, recorded June 3, 1985, broadcast Radio 3, March 4, 1986.
Fraser, G.S., *The Modern Writer and His World: Continuity and Innovation in Twentieth Century English Literature*, Frederick A. Praeger, New York, 1953, pp. 302-303, 346-350.
- 'The Poetry of Thom Gunn', *Critical Quarterly*, 3:4, Manchester, Winter, 1961, pp. 359-367.
- *Metre, Rhyme and Free Verse*, Methuen, London, 1970, pp. 51, 57-58.
Fuller, John, 'Thom Gunn', in Ian Hamilton, ed. *The Modern Writer: Essays from the Review*, MacDonald, London, 1968, pp. 17-22.
Galloway, David and Christian Sabisch, eds., *Calamus: Male Homosexuality in Twentieth Century Literature*, William Morrow, New York, 1982, pp. 491-492.
Gewanter, David, 'A Different Formalism: Thom Gunn's "Lament"', *Agni*, 36, Boston, Massachusetts, 1992, pp. 307-309.
Giles, Paul, 'Landscapes of Repetition: the Self-Parodic Nature of Thom Gunn's Later Poetry', *Critical Quarterly*, 29:2, Manchester, Summer, 1987, pp. [85]-99.
- 'From Myth to History: the Later Poetry of Thom Gunn and Ted Hughes', in James Acheson and Romana Huk, eds., *Contemporary British Poetry: Essays in Theory and Criticism*, State University of New York Press, Albany, New York, 1996.
Glazier, Lyle, 'Thom Gunn', *Credences*, 3:2, Buffalo, New York, Spring, 1985, pp. 155-162.
Goerling, Fritz, 'Thom Gunn', in Horst W. Drescher, *Englische Literatur der Gegenwart*, Alfred Kroner Verlag, Stuttgart, 1970, pp. [567]-578 (in German).
Goto, Maisei, 'Kyo Kaijin Thom Gunn', *Eigo Seinen*, 125:2, Tokyo, May 1, 1979, pp. 7-10 (in Japanese).

Green, Peter, 'Thou Art Translated: The Surprising Revival of the *Metamorphoses*', *Times Literary Supplement*, 4787, December 30, 1994, pp. 3-4.
Gross, Harvey, *Sound and Form in Modern Poetry*, University of Michigan Press, Ann Arbor, MI, 1964, p. 35.
Grubb, Frederick, *A Vision of Reality: a Study of Literature in Twentieth Century Verse*, Chatto and Windus, London, 1965, pp. 54, 78, 193, 202-213, 217, 226, 240.
Hewitt, Jerene, 'Poet of the Year, 1979: Thom Gunn', *Inscape 79: an Anthology*, 35, Pasadena City College, California, May 1, 1979, p. 40.
Haffenden, John, *Viewpoints: Poets in Conversation*, Faber, London, 1981, pp. 35-36.
Hall, Donald, '1988 Robert Kirsch Award', *Los Angeles Times Book Review*, California, November 6, 1988, pp. 1-2 / reprinted as 'Thom Gunn Resisting' in Donald Hall, *Death to the Death of Poetry: Essays, Reviews, Notes, Interviews*, University of Michigan Press, Ann Arbor, MI, 1994, pp. 27-31.
– 'Thom Gunn', *PN Review*, 70, 16:2, Manchester, 1989, pp. 29-30.
Hamilton, Ian, 'The Making of the Movement', *New Statesman*, 81:2092, London, November, 1964, pp. 64-70.
Hartley, Anthony, 'Poets of the Fifties', *Spectator*, 6682, London, July 20, 1952), pp. 100-101.
Hassan, Salem Kadheim, *Time, Tense and Structure in Contemporary English Poetry: Larkin, and the Movement*, PhD thesis, University of Glasgow, 1985.
Haya, Kenichi, 'Thom Gunn No Shi', *Eigo Seinen* (Tokyo), 117, Tokyo, April 1, 1971, pp. 16-17 (in Japanese).
Hinton, Brian, *The Poetry of Thom Gunn*, MA thesis, University of Birmingham, 1975.
Holbrook, David, 'The Cult of Hughes and Gunn: the Dangers of Poetical Fashion', *Poetry Review*, 54:2, London, Summer, 1963), pp. 167-183.
Homberger, Eric, *The Art of the Real: Poetry in England and America since 1939*, Dent, London, 1977, pp. 72, 94, 95, 96, 182.
Hulse, Michael, 'The Repossession of Innocence: the Poetry of Thom Gunn', *Quadrant*, 27:4, Sydney, April, 1983, pp. 65-69.
Hunter, Jim, ed., *Modern Poets Four*, revised edition, Faber, London, 1979, pp. 59-60, 77-80.
Ivasheva, V, 'The Struggle is Not Over: on the Aesthetics of English Modernism', *Inostrannaya Literatura*, 5, Moscow, 1959, pp. 180-189 (in Russian).
Ivasheva, V, 'Modern English Poetry', *Voprosy Literatura*, 9, Moscow, 1966, pp. 183-197 (in Russian).
Izzo, Carlo, ed., *Poesia Inglese del '900*, Guanda, Parma, 1967, p. 891 (in Italian).
Jennings, Elizabeth, *Poetry Today*, Longmans, Green & Co., London, 1961, p. 42.
Jones, Peter, and Michael Schmidt, eds., *British Poetry Since 1970: a Critical Survey*, Carcanet, Manchester, 1980, pp. x, xv, xix, xxiii, xxiv, 46, 138-140, 150, 153.
Kennedy, James G., 'The Two European Cultures and the Necessary New Sense of Literature', *College English*, 31:6, Champaign, Illinois, March, 1970, pp. 571-602.
Kettle, A. 'English Literature in 1955', *Inostrannaya Literatura*, 4, Moscow, 1956, pp. 219-229 (in Russian).
King, Jenny, 'I Entered by the Darkened Door', in William Zaranka, ed., *The Brand-X Anthology of Poetry: a Parody Anthology*, Applewood Books, Cambridge, Massachusetts, 1981, p. 335.
King, P.R., *Nine Contemporary Poets: a Critical Introduction*, Methuen, London, 1979, pp. 77-106.
Klawitter, George, 'Piety and the Agnostic Gay Poet: Thom Gunn's Biblical Homoerotics', in Raymond Jean Frontain, ed., *Reclaiming the Sacred: the Bible in Gay and Lesbian Culture*, Haworth, New York, 1997.

Kleinzahler, August, 'The Plain Style and the City', *Agenda*, 37:2-3, London, Autumn-Winter, 1999, pp. 36-48.

Landau, Deborah, 'How to Live, What to Do: the Poetics and Politics of AIDS', *American Literature: a Journal of Literary History, Criticism and Bibliography*, 68:1, Durham, North Carolina, March, 1996, pp. 193-225.

Leider, Emily, 'Thom Gunn in California', *San Francisco Review of Books*, 7:5, California, January-February, 1983, pp. 17-18.

Lesniak, James, G., ed., *Contemporary Authors: New Revision Series*, 33, Gale Research Inc., Detroit, MI, 1991, pp. 195-197.

Lesser, Wendy, *The Life Below Ground: a Study of the Subterranean in Literature and History*, Faber, Boston, Massachusetts and London, 1987, pp. 55-61.

- 'Autobiography and the "I" of the Beholder', *New York Times Book Review*, 1, New York, November 27, 1988, pp. 26-28.
- 'Thom Gunn', *Agenda*, 37:2-3, London, Autumn-Winter, 1999, pp. 118-122.

Levin, Jonathan, 'Thom Gunn', in George Strade and Carol Howard, eds., *British Writers*, Supplement IV, Scribners, New York.

Link, Viktor, '"Diagrams" und "Iron Landscapes": Tradition und Wandel in Thom Gunns Gedichten', in Karl Josef Höltgen, Lothar Hönighausen, Eberhard Kreuzer and Gotz Schmitz, eds., *Tradition und Innovation in der Englischen und Amerikanischen Lyrik des 20 Jahrhunderts*, Max Niemayer Verlag, Tübingen, 1986 (in German).

Logan, William, 'A Letter from Britain', Part II, *Poetry*, 157:5, Chicago, February, 1991, pp. 290-299.

Lombardo, Agostino, 'Thom Gunn e il Nuovo Movimento', in *Thom Gunn i Miei Tristi Capitani e Altre Poesie*, Arnoldo Mondadori Editore, Milan, 1968, pp. 7-25.

Lucie-Smith, Edward, ed., *British Poetry Since 1945*, Penguin, Middlesex, 1970, p. 143.

- 'Poets in Conference', *Encounter*, 26:6, London, June, 1966, pp. 41-42.
- 'The Tortured Yearned as Well: an Enquiry into Themes of Cruelty in Current Verse', *Critical Quarterly*, 4:1, Manchester, Spring, 1962, pp. 38-43.

Maizels, S., 'Imagined Foes', *Inostrannaya Literatura*, 12, Moscow, 1957, pp. 258-259 (in Russian).

Mander, John, *The Writer and Commitment*, Secker and Warburg, London, 1961, pp. 14, 19-20, 43, 153-178, 179, 180, 211.

Martin, Robert Kessler, *The Half-Hid Warp: Whitman, Crane, and the Tradition of 'Adhesiveness' in American Poetry*, PhD thesis, Brown University, Providence, RI, 1978.

- *The Homosexual Tradition in American Poetry*, University of Texas Press, Austin, Texas, 1979, pp. 165, 179-190, 229.
- 'Fetishizing America: David Hockney and Thom Gunn', in Robert K. Martin, ed., *The Continuing Presence of Walt Whitman: the Life After the Life*, University of Iowa Press, Iowa, 1992, pp. [114]-126.

McPheron, William, 'Thom Gunn', in *First Drafts, Last Drafts: Forty Years of the Creative Writing Program at Stanford*, Stanford University Libraries, California, 1989, p. 26.

Megerle, Brenda Powell, *Contemporary Poets: the Quest for Value Beyond Nihilism*, PhD thesis, University of California, Berkeley, California, 1980, pp. [155]-188.

Miglior, Giorgio, 'La Poesia di Thom Gunn', in Claudio Gorlier, ed., *Studi e Ricerchi di Letterratura Inglese e Americana*, II, Cisalpino-Goliardica, 1969, pp. [21]-51.

Miller, John, 'The Stipulative Imagination of Thom Gunn', *Iowa Review*, 4:1, Iowa, Winter, 1973, pp. 54-72.

Miller, Karl, F.C., 'Profile: Thom Gunn: Cambridge Poet', *Varsity*, Cambridge, October 18, 1952, p. 4.

- 'Cambridge Writing of Last Year', *Chequer*, 3, Cambridge, November, 1953, pp. 32-35.

Mitgutsch, Waltraud, *Zur Lyrik von Ted Hughes und Thom Gunn: eine Interpretation Nach Leitmotiven,* PhD thesis, Universitat Salzburg, 1973 (in German).
– 'Thom Gunn', *Salzburg Studies in English Literature,* 27, Salzburg, 27, 1974, pp. 170-199 (in German).
Moore, Geoffrey, *Poetry Today,* Longmans, Green & Co., London, 1958, pp. 45-47, 53-54.
Morrison, Blake, *The Movement: English Poetry and Fiction of the 1950s,* Oxford University Press, Oxford, 1980, pp. 2-4, 6-7, 9, 29-32, 40-43, 45, 47, 50, 57, 65, 68-69, 96, 99, 118-120, 135, 169, 184-189, 193, 217, 219, 247-248, 252, 274-275, 277-278, 282.
– 'The Movement and its Audience', *Times Literary Supplement,* 4019, London, April 4, 1980, pp. 393-395.
– 'Young Poets in the 1970s', in Peter Jones and Michael Schmidt, eds., *British Poetry Since 1970: a Critical Survey,* Carcanet, Manchester, 1980, pp. [141]-156.
– 'Thom Gunn', in Vincent B. Sherry, *Dictionary of Literary Biography,* 27, Gale Research Inc., Detroit, Michigan, 1984, pp. 117-129.
O'Connor, William Van, *The New University Wits and the End of Modernism,* Southern Illinois University Press, Carbondale, Illinois, 1963, pp. 6, 7, 77, 103, 120, 126-130, 154.
Okeke-Ezigbo, Emika, 'Moore's "To a Snail" and Gunn's "Considering the Snail"', *Explicator,* 42:2, Washington, Winter, 1984, pp. 17-18.
Oppel, Horst, ed., 'Thom Gunn', in *In the Tank: Die Moderne Englische Lyrik: Interpretation,* Eric Schmidt Verlag, Berlin, 1967, pp. 317-324 (in German).
Osborne, Charles, 'A Rhyme of Poets: a Diary of Last Week's Poetry International Festival', *Sunday Times,* London, July 5, 1970, p. 27.
Ousby, Ian, ed., *The Cambridge Guide to Literature in English,* Cambridge University Press, Cambridge, 1992, revised p/b edition, p. 422.
Parini, Jay, 'Rule and Energy: the Poetry of Thom Gunn', *Massachusetts Review,* 23:1, Amherst, Massachusetts, Spring, 1982, pp. 134-151.
Pearson, Gabriel, 'Romanticism and Contemporary Poetry', *New Left Review,* 16, London, July-August, 1962, pp. 47-75.
Peck, John, 'On Two Stanzas by Thom Gunn', *PN Review,* 70, 16:2, Manchester, Autumn, 1989, pp. 35-36.
Pennati, Camillo, Introduction, *Almanaco dello Specchio,* 3, Milan, 1974, pp. 145-147.
Perkins, David, *A History of Modern Poetry,* Harvard University Press, Cambridge, Massachusetts, 1987, pp. 12, 349, 419, 422, 424, 446, 447, 449, 463-470, 537.
Pinsky, Robert, 'Thom Gunn', *PN Review,* 70, 16:2, Manchester, Autumn, 1989, pp. 42-43.
– 'The Lenore Marshall/*Nation* Poetry Prize – 1993', *Nation,* 257:19, December 6, 1993, pp. 701-703.
Powell, Neil, 'The Abstract Joy: Thom Gunn's Early Poetry', *Critical Quarterly,* 13:3, Manchester, Autumn, 1971, [219]-227.
– *Tradition and Structure in Contemporary Poetry: Thom Gunn, Donald Davie, Philip Larkin,* MPhil thesis, University of Warwick, Coventry, 1974.
– 'Loud Music, Bars and Boisterous Men', *PN Review,* 70, 16:2, Manchester, Autumn, 1989, pp. 39-41.
Press, John, 'English Verse Since 1945', in Peter Green, ed., *Essays by Diverse Hands,* 31, Oxford University Press, Oxford, 1962, pp. [143]-184.
– *Rule and Energy: Trends in British Poetry Since the Second World War,* Oxford University Press, London, 1963, pp. 3, 44, 56, 160, 235, 191-201.
– *A Map of Modern English Verse,* Oxford University Press, London, 1969, pp. 234-235, 251, 253, 254, 255-256, 263-264.
Pritchard, William H., *Seeing Through Everything: English Writers, 1918-1940,* Faber, London, 1977, p. 169.

Rexroth, Kenneth, 'The New American Poets', *Harper's Magazine,* 230:1381, New York, June, 1965, pp. [65]-71.

Ries, Lawrence R., *Wolf Masks: Violence in Contemporary Poetry,* Kennikat Press, Port Washington, New York, 1977, pp. 7-8, 12-13, 18-20, 22-24, 42, 51, 56, 59-91, 92-93, 95, 99, 125, 153-154.

Robinson, Marion, *'And Now We Have the Movement, Mostly Still': a Study of a Group of Contemporary Poets,* PhD thesis, University of Exeter, Devon, 1964.

Romer, Stephen, 'Thom Gunn: a Story of Hero-Worship and Beyond ...', *Agenda,* 37:2-3, London, Autumn-Winter, 1999, pp. 31-35.

Roper, Derek, 'Tradition and Innovation in the Occidental Lyric of the Last Decade: I: English Poetry and the Tradition, 1950-1960', *Books Abroad,* 34:4, Autumn, 1960, Norman, Oklahoma, pp. [344]-348.

Rosenthal, M.L., *The New Poets: American and British Poetry Since World War II,* Oxford University Press, New York, 1967, pp. 194, 199, 251-257.

Rückert, Ingrid, *The Touch of Sympathy: Philip Larkin und Thom Gunn: Zwei Beiträge zur Englischen Gegenwartsdichtung,* Carl Winter Universitats-Verlag, Heidelberg, 1982 (in German).

Sagar, Keith, *The Art of Ted Hughes,* Cambridge University Press, Cambridge, 1975, pp. 13, 175-176, 181, 196.

Sarver, Tony, 'Thom Gunn', *Gay News,* 134, London, January 12-25, 1978, pp. 16, 26.

Schmidt, Michael, and Grevel Lindop, eds., *British Poetry Since 1960: a Critical Survey,* Carcanet, Oxford, 1972, pp. 72, 73, 235, 236-239.

– 'Gunn, for Example', *PN Review,* 70, 16:2, Manchester, Autumn, 1989, p. 37.

– *Lives of the Poets,* Weidenfeld & Nicolson, London, 1998, pp. 2, 10, 152, 187, 369, 490, 599, 622, 668, 670, 721, 729, 733-737, 789, 792, 807, 882.

Seehase, Georg, 'The Sense of Movement: Über den Aktionsraum des Lyrischen Helden in Einigen Werken Englischer Gegenwartsdichtung', *Zeitschrift für Anglistik und Amerikanistik,* 1, Leipzig, January, 1970, pp. 71-87 (in German).

Seymour-Smith, Martin, *Who's Who in Twentieth Century Literature,* McGraw Hill, New York, 1977, p. 146.

Sherwood, Matt, 'The Head and Heart of Gunn's Work', *In Other Words,* 2:7, Amherst College, Massachusetts, May 8, 1981, p. 9.

Sinfield, Alan, *Literature, Culture and Politics in Postwar Britain,* Basil Blackwell, Oxford, 1989, pp. 81-84, 92, 168-169, 183, 192, 283.

Sloan, LaRue Love, 'Gunn's "On the Move"', *Explicator,* 46:3, Washington, Spring, 1988, pp. 44-48.

Smith, A.J.P., *Brodie's Notes on* Thom Gunn and Ted Hughes: Selected Poems, Pan Books, London, 1980, pp. [5]-25.

Sola Buil, Ricardo, *La Actitud Poetica de Philip Larkin, Ted Hughes y Thom Gunn,* MA thesis, University of Zaragoza, 1972 (in Spanish).

Stimpson, Catharine R., 'Thom Gunn: the Redefinition of Place', *Contemporary Literature,* 18:3, Madison, Wisconsin, Summer, 1977, pp. [391]-404.

Swaab, Peter, '*The Man with Night Sweats* and the Idea of Political Poetry', *Agenda,* 37:2-3, London, Autumn-Winter, 1999, pp. 107-113.

Symons, Julian, 'Thom Gunn', in James Vinson, ed., *Contemporary Poets,* second edition, St James Press, London, 1975, pp. 605-608.

Temple, John, 'Thoughts on the Teaching, Learning, and Study of Literature', in J.P. Vander, ed., *Elizabethan and Modern Studies,* Seminarie voor Engelse en Amerikaanse Literatura, RUG, Ghent, 1985, pp. 257-266.

Thirlby, Peter, 'Thom Gunn – Violence and Toughness', *Delta,* 8, Cambridge, Spring, 1956, pp. 16-21.

Thwaite, Anthony, *Contemporary English Poetry: an Introduction*, Heinemann, London, 1964, pp. 143-166.
– *Poetry Today: 1960-1973*, Longman, Essex, 1973, pp. 33, 40-41.
Tomlinson, Charles, 'Some Presences on the Scene: a Vista of Postwar Poetry', in Vereen Bell and Laurence Lerner, eds., *On Modern Poetry: Essays Presented to Donald Davie*, Vanderbilt University, Tennessee, 1988, pp. 213-232.
Twose, Gareth, *The Relationship Between Book Sales and Reviews, with Reference to Thom Gunn*, MA thesis, Manchester University, 1992.
Untermeyer, Louis, ed., *50 Modern American and British Poets, 1920-1970*, David McKay, New York, 1973, pp. 333-334.
Vince, Michael, 'Helping Us See: a View of "From the Wave"', *Agenda*, 37:2-3, London, Autumn-Winter, 1999, pp. 98-101.
Wakeman, John, ed., *World Authors, 1950-1970: a Companion Volume to Twentieth Century Authors*, The H.W. Wilson Co., New York, 1975, pp. 602-603.
Wall, Alan, 'Gunn, Thom', in James Vinson, ed., *Great Writers of the English Language: Poets*, St Martin's Press, New York, 1979, pp. 445-447.
Wasserburg, Charles, 'Angels, Atheists and Evangelists', *Southern Review*, 28:2, Baton Rouge, Louisiana, April, 1992, pp. 371-389.
Weiner, Joshua, 'Gunn's "Meat": Notations on Craft', *Agni*, 36, Boston, Massachusetts, October, 1992, pp. 303-306.
Wells, Robert, '"Images of Life": the Poetry of Thom Gunn', *Agenda*, 37:2-3, London, Autumn-Winter, 1999, pp. 22-30.
Wilmer, Clive, 'Clive Wilmer on Thom Gunn', *Granta*, 73:1247, Cambridge, April 22, 1967, pp. 20-21.
– 'Definition and Flow: a Personal Reading of Thom Gunn', *PN Review*, 7, 5:3, Manchester, May, 1978, pp. 51-57.
– Introduction, *PN Review*, 70, 16:2, Manchester, Autumn, 1989, p. 26.
– '"Those Wounds Heal Ill": Thom Gunn in 1954 and 1992', *Agenda*, 37:2-3, London, Autumn-Winter, 1999, pp. 13-21.
Winters, Yvor, *Forms of Discovery*, Alan Swallow, Denver, Colorado, 1967, pp. 343-345, 349-350.
Woodcock, Bruce, *Thom Gunn and Michel Foucault*, Bete Noir, Hull.
– '"But Oh Not Loose": Form and Sexuality in Thom Gunn's Poetry', *Critical Quarterly*, 35:1, London, Spring, 1993, pp. 60-72.
Woods, Gregory, *Articulate Flesh: Male Homo-Eroticism and Modern Poetry*, Yale University Press, New Haven, Connecticut, 1987, pp. 32, 71, 105, 109, 111, 118, [212]-231.
– 'The Sniff of the Real', *Agenda*, 37:2-3, London, Autumn-Winter, 1999, pp. 92-97.
Woolman, Maurice, ed., *Ten Contemporary Poets*, George G. Harrap, London, 1963, p. 65.
Wynne-Davies, Marion, *Bloomsbury Guide to English Literature*, Bloomsbury, London, 1989, p. 578.
Zamora, Edward, *A Critical Analysis of Thom Gunn's Selected Poems, 1950-1975*, MA thesis, Texas A and I University, Kingsville, Texas, 1983.

Reviews

Books and Pamphlets by TG

Thom Gunn (Fantasy Press, 1953)

Thwaite, Anthony, Untitled, *Trio,* 4, Oxford, October, 1953, pp. 21-22.
Hill, High C., Untitled, *Outposts,* 25, London, 1954, pp. 18-19 Omnibus Review.
Anonymous, 'The Shield of Irony', *Times Literary Supplement,* 2722, London, April 2, 1954, p. 218, Omnibus Review.

Fighting Terms (Fantasy Press, 1954)

Jones, David, 'Cambridge Poetry', *Varsity,* Cambridge University, Cambridge, June 5, 1954, p. 8, Omnibus Review.
Miller, Karl, 'Thom Gunn's "Fighting Terms"', *Granta,* 57:1147, Cambridge, June 8, 1954, pp. 27-29.
Ridler, Anne, 'Two Poets', *Manchester Guardian,* Manchester, July 30, 1954, p. 4, Omnibus Review.
Fraser, G.S., 'Texture and Structure', *New Statesman and Nation,* 48:1221, London, July 31, 1954, pp. 137-138, Omnibus Review.
Hartley, Anthony, 'Poets of the Fifties', *Spectator,* 193:6583, London, August 27, 1954, pp. 260-261, Omnibus Review.
Ward, David E., Untitled, *Delta,* Cambridge, Autumn, 1954, unpaginated, Omnibus Review.
Anonymous, 'Plain Speech and Pedantry', *Times Literary Supplement,* 2755, London, November 19, 1954, p. 741, Omnibus Review.
Bergonzi, Bernard, Untitled, *Listen,* 1:3, Hessle, Yorkshire, Winter, 1954, pp. 21-23, Omnibus Review.
Michie, James, Untitled, *London Magazine,* 2:1, London, January, 1955, pp. 96, 99-100, Omnibus Review.
Enright, D.J., 'Verse: Hard and Soft', *Month,* 15:5, London, June, 1956, pp. 372-373, Omnibus Review.

Fighting Terms (Hawk's Well Press, 1958)

Alvarez, Alfred, 'Poetry Chronicle', *Partisan Review,* 25:4, New York, Autumn, 1958, pp. 603-609, Omnibus Review.
Simpson, Louis, 'In the Absence of Yeats', *Hudson Review,* 12:2, New York, Summer, 1959, pp. [308]-314, Omnibus Review.
Anonymous, 'Poetry', *Gazette,* Weekender Magazine, Berkeley, California, July 6, 1963, p. 12, Omnibus Review.

Fighting Terms (Faber and Faber, 1962)

Connolly, Cyril, 'The Shadow of Parnassus', *Sunday Times,* London, March 4, 1962, p. 31, Omnibus Review.
Lykiard, Alexis, 'Poetry', *Granta,* 65:1216, Cambridge, March 10, 1962, pp. 35-36.
Alvarez, A, 'Tuning into a New Voice', *Observer,* Weekend Review, London, March 11,

1962, p. 29, Omnibus Review.
Causley, Charles, 'An Assured Talent', *Birmingham Post*, Birmingham, March 13, 1962, p. 3, Omnibus Review.
Anonymous, 'A Narrative Poet', *Irish Times*, Dublin, March 24, 1962, p. 8, Omnibus Review.
Evans, Eric, 'Mr Comfort and Mr Gunn', *Oxford Times*, Oxford, April 13, 1962, p. 26, Omnibus Review.
Anonymous, Untitled, *Books and Bookmen*, 7:7, London, April, 1962, p. 54.
Fuller, John, 'Thom Gunn', *the Review*, 1, London, April-May, 1962, pp. 29-34.
Davie, Donald, 'Reason Revealed', *New Statesman*, 63:1625, London, May 4, 1962, pp. 639-640, Omnibus Review.
Dale, Peter, Untitled, *Agenda*, 2:7-8, May-June, 1962, pp. 21-[25], Omnibus Review.
Press, John, Untitled, *Cambridge Review*, 83:2032, Cambridge, June 16, 1962, pp. 539-540.
Fried, Michael, Untitled, *London Magazine*, 2:3, London, June, 1962, pp. 85-87.
Anonymous, 'Poets, People, Victorian Cameos and a Walking Pond', *Times*, London, July 5, 1962, p. 17, Omnibus Review.
Jennings, Elizabeth, 'Poems and Re-creations', *Daily Telegraph*, London, July 20, 1962, p. 17, Omnibus Review.
Sealy, Douglas, Untitled, *Dublin Magazine*, 1:4, Dublin, August, 1962, pp. 67-68.
Skelton, Robin, Untitled, *Critical Quarterly*, 4:3, London, Autumn, 1962, pp. 274-276, Omnibus Review.
Boyer, Peter B., Untitled, *Osmania Journal of English Studies*, 2, Hyderabad, 1962, p. 84.
Wood, Christopher, 'Current Literature 1962, I: Prose, Poetry and Drama', *English Studies*, 44:1-6, Amsterdam, 1963, pp. 222-233, Omnibus Review.

THE SENSE OF MOVEMENT (Faber and Faber, 1957)

Betjeman, John, 'Round the Poets' Gallery', *Daily Telegraph*, London, June 7, 1957, p. 12, Omnibus Review.
Anonymous, 'Wrenching Values', *Times Literary Supplement*, 2885, London, June 14, 1957, p. 360, Omnibus Review.
Conquest, Robert, 'A Major New Poet?', *Spectator*, 198:6729, London, June 14, 1957, pp. 786-787, Omnibus Review.
Alvarez, A., 'Signs of Poetic Life', *Observer*, London, June 16, 1957, p. 19, Omnibus Review.
Press, John, 'Tough and Tender', *Sunday Times*, London, June 16, 1957, p. 8.
Anonymous, Untitled, *Listener*, 58:1475, London, July 4, 1957, p. 25, Omnibus Review.
Ridler, Anne, 'Verses of the Season', *Manchester Guardian*, July 5, 1957, p. 7, Omnibus Review.
Ferguson, Peter, 'New Poems', *Isis*, 1301, Oxford, July 13, 1957, pp. 29, 31, Omnibus Review.
Muir, Edwin, 'Time and Place', *New Statesman*, 54:1374, London, July 13, 1957, pp. 59-60, Omnibus Review.
E.E., 'Vehicle of Transport', *Oxford Times*, Oxford, July 19, 1957, p. 16.
Gillett, Eric, 'Books New and Old: a Quiver of Lives', *National and English Review*, London, July, 1957, pp. 31-34, Omnibus Review.
Fallon, Padraic, 'Verse Chronicle', *Dublin Magazine*, 32:3, Dublin, July-September, 1957, pp. 43-47, Omnibus Review.
Scott, Alexander, 'A Growing Scottish Talent', *Glasgow Herald*, Glasgow, August 8, 1957, p. 3, Omnibus Review.
Abse, Dannie, 'New Poetry', *Time and Tide*, 38:32, London, August 10, 1957, p. 1000,

Omnibus Review.
Press, John, 'Modern Poets in Search of a Public', *Times*, London, August 15, 1957, p. 11, Omnibus Review.
Hall, J.C., '"Gay She Was As a Pin Table"', *Books and Bookmen*, 2:12, London, September, 1957, p. 30, Omnibus Review.
Holloway, John, Untitled, *London Magazine,* 4:9, London, September, 1957, pp. 69-73, Omnibus Review.
Levenson, Christopher, 'Vigour Within the Discipline of Shape', *Delta*, 13, Cambridge, Autumn, 1957, pp. 27-30.
Hough, Graham, 'Landmarks and Turbulence', *Encounter*, 9:5, London, November, 1957, pp. 83-84, 86-87, Omnibus Review.
Sergeant, Howard, Untitled, *Outposts,* 35, London, Winter, 1957-1958, pp. 17-19.
Mathias, Roland, Untitled, *Dock Leaves,* 8:22, Pembroke Dock, Wales, 1957, pp. 56-61, Omnibus Review.
Armstrong, Robert, 'Ebb and Flow', *Poetry Review*, 49:1, London, January-March, 1958, pp. 41-42, Omnibus Review.
Kermode, Frank, 'The Problem of Pleasure', *Listen,* 2:4, Hessle, Yorkshire, Spring, 1958, pp. 14-19, Omnibus Review.
Morse, Samuel French, 'A Transatlantic View', *Poetry*, 92:5, Chicago, Illinois, August, 1958, pp. 318-329, Omnibus Review.

The Sense of Movement (University of Chicago Press, 1954)

Hogan, William, 'A Bookman's Notebook – New Stegner Novella: Other News and Notes', *San Francisco Chronicle,* California, March 31, 1959, p. 33, Omnibus Review.
Derelith, August, Untitled, *Capital Times,* Madison, Wisconsin, April 2, 1959, p. 23.
Henderson, Nat, Untitled, *American Statesman,* Austin, Texas, May 10, 1959, p. C3.
Holley, Fred S., 'Poets Speak with Dignity', *Virginian Pilot and Portsmouth Star,* Norfolk, Virginia, May 10, 1959, p. 6F.
Booth, Philip, 'Gunn and Snodgrass', *Christian Science Monitor,* Boston, Massachusetts, May 14, 1959, pp. [503]-509, Omnibus Review.
Brady, Charles A., '10 New Volumes Show Quality of Modern Poetry', *Buffalo Evening News,* Buffalo, New York, June 13, 1959, p. B-6, Omnibus Review.
Anderson, Carl, 'Poetry Collections, Elegant and Ironic', *Dallas Times Herald*, Dallas, Texas, June 21, 1959, p. 17, Omnibus Review.
Jacobsen, Josephine, 'Selected New Books in Review: an Anthology and Two Poets', *Evening Sun,* Baltimore, Maryland, June 29, 1959, p. 18, Omnibus Review.
Fitts, Dudley, 'New Verse for Midsummer Night Dreamers', *Saturday Review of Literature*, 42:30, New York, July 25, 1959, pp. 14-16, Omnibus Review.
Meredith, William, 'In the "I" of the Poet', *New York Times Book Review*, New York, July 26, 1959, p. 25, Omnibus Review.
Kohler, Dayton, 'Authentic Achievement of Three Poets', *Courier-Journal*, Louisville, Kentucky, July 26, 1959, Section 4, p. 7, Omnibus Review.
Jerome, Judson, 'Poets of the Sixties', *Antioch Review*, 19:3, Yellow Springs, Ohio, Autumn, 1959, pp. 421-432, Omnibus Review.
Thompson, John, 'A Poetry Chronicle', *Poetry*, 95:2, Chicago, Illinois, November, 1959, pp. 107-116, Omnibus Review.
Becker, John E., 'The Sense of Movement: Poems', *Catholic Review Service*, 10:52, St Mary's, Kansas, December 29, 1959, pp. 295-296.
Dickey, James, 'The Suspect in Poetry or Everyman as Detective', *Sewanee Review,* 68:4, Sewanee, Tennessee, October-December, 1960, pp. 660-674, Omnibus Review.

Talbot, Norman, '... From America', *Poetry Australia*, 1:6, Sydney, October, 1965, p. 40, Omnibus Review.
McConathy, Dale, 'The Poet and the Jukebox', *Harper's Bazaar*, 100:3050, New York, January, 1966, pp. 84, 165, Omnibus Review.

MY SAD CAPTAINS (Faber and Faber, 1961)

Tanner, Tony, 'An Armour of Concepts', *Time and Tide*, 42:35, London, August 31, 1961, pp. 140-141.
Bergonzi, Bernard, 'A Mythologizing Tendency', *Manchester Guardian*, Manchester, September 1, 1961, p. 5, Omnibus Review.
Evans, Eric, 'Thom Gunn', *Oxford Times*, Oxford, September 1, 1961, p. 22.
Thwaite, Anthony, 'Good, Bad and Chaos', *Spectator*, 207:6949, London, September 1, 1961, pp. 298-299, Omnibus Review.
Press, John, 'Struggle of the Human Spirit', *Sunday Times Magazine*, London, September 3, 1961, p. 25, Omnibus Review.
Ricks, Christopher, 'Not So Tough', *Sunday Telegraph*, London, September 3, 1961, p. 6, Omnibus Review.
Greacen, Robert, 'Greek Grandeur', *Daily Telegraph*, London, September 8, 1961, p. 16, Omnibus Review.
Alvarez, A, 'The Poet of the Black Jackets', *Observer*, London, September 10, 1961, p. 24, Omnibus Review.
Barry, Gerald, Barbara Bray, Richard Mayne, Eric Newton, Edgar Anstey, Richard Findlater, *The Critics*, BBC Home Programme Broadcast, September 10, 1961, transcript, recording TL063390.
Anonymous, 'Candour, Clarity and Compassion in Modern Verse', *Times*, London, September 28, 1961, p. 15, Omnibus Review.
Anonymous, 'An Authentic Talent', *Times Literary Supplement*, 3109, London, September 29, 1961, p. 646.
Kermode, Frank, 'Towards Transparency', *New Statesman*, 62:1595, London, October 6, 1961, pp. 479-480, Omnibus Review.
Clarke, Austin, 'The Quality of Thought', *Irish Times*, Dublin, October 7, 1961, p. 8, Omnibus Review.
Furbank, P.N., 'New Poetry', *Listener*, 66:1698, London, October 12, 1961, p. 575, Omnibus Review.
C., J., 'Books of Verse', *Belfast News Letter*, Belfast, October 18, 1961, p. 3, Omnibus Review.
Lovelock, Yann, 'Recent Poetry', *Isis*, 1399, Oxford, October 18, 1961, p. 22, Omnibus Review.
Anonymous, Untitled, *Granta*, 65:1211, Cambridge, October 21, 1961, p. 20, Omnibus Review.
Robson, Jeremy, 'Emotion and Efficiency', *Tribune*, London, October 27, 1961, p. 10, Omnibus Review.
Anonymous, 'Poet's Themes: Solitude, Faith and Time', *Scotsman*, Edinburgh, November 18, 1961, Weekend Magazine, p. 2, Omnibus Review.
Fried, Michael, 'A Question of Form', *New Left Review*, 12, London, November-December, 1961, pp. 68-70, Omnibus Review.
Chiari, J., 'Lettres et Arts: L'Actualité Poétique', BBC French Broadcast, London, December 4, 1961, Transcript.
Young, Douglas, 'Harvest of Verse', *Glasgow Herald*, Glasgow, December 7, 1961, Christmas Book Supplement, p. 3, Omnibus Review.

Alvarez, A., 'Books of the Year', *Observer*, London, December 17, 1961, p. 22, Omnibus Review.
Anonymous, 'Recent Poetry', *Yorkshire Post*, Leeds, December 21, 1961, p. 4, Omnibus Review.
Dickinson, Peter, 'How It Is with the Muse', *Punch*, 241:6329, London, December 27, 1961, p. 953, Omnibus Review.
Broadbent, J.B., 'My Sad Captains', *Delta*, 25, Cambridge, Winter, 1961, pp. 26-30.
Dyson, A.E., Untitled, *Critical Quarterly*, 3:4, London, Winter, 1961, pp. 377-380, Omnibus Review.
Rathmell, J.C.A., Untitled, *Cambridge Review*, 83:2018, Cambridge, January 27, 1962, pp. 233, 235.
Forman, Joan, 'Veins of Ore', *Poetry Review*, 53:1, London, January-March, 1962, p. 41, Omnibus Review.
Lucie-Smith, Edward, 'The Tortured Yearned As Well: Enquiry into Themes of Cruelty in Current Verse', *Critical Quarterly*, 4:1, London, Spring, 1962, pp. 34-43, Omnibus Review.
Tomlinson, Charles, 'Poets and Mushrooms: a Retrospect of British Poetry in 1961', *Poetry*, 100:2, Chicago, Illinois, May, 1962, pp. 104-121, Omnibus Review.
Mathias, Roland, Untitled, *Anglo-Welsh Review*, 12:29, Pembroke Dock, Wales, 1962, pp. 65-70.
Dale, Peter, Untitled, *Agenda*, 2:7-8, London, May-June, 1962, pp. 21-[25], Omnibus Review.
Sergeant, Howard, 'Poetry Review', *English*, 14:80, London, Summer, 1962, pp. 73-75, Omnibus Review.
Ghose, Zulfikar, 'Still Seeking a Voice of His Own', *Western Daily Press & Bristol Mirror*, Bristol, October 22, 1962, p. 4, Omnibus Review.
Rodway, Allan, 'Existence Before Essence: Six Poets', *Listen*, 4:1, Hessle, Yorkshire, Autumn, 1962, pp. 24-28, Omnibus Review.
Jackson, Robert, Untitled, *Outposts*, 51, London, Winter, 1962, pp. 24-25, Omnibus Review.

MY SAD CAPTAINS (University of Chicago Press, 1961)

Robie, Burton A., 'Poetry', *Library Journal*, 88:17, Chicago, Illinois, October 1, 1961, p. 3286, Omnibus Review.
Smith, Hal, 'Notes, Reviews, Speculations', *Epoch*, 11:3, Ithaca, New York, Autumn, 1961, pp. 187-190, Omnibus Review.
Schevill, James, 'Contemporary Poetry – Lowell, Wilbur, Gunn, and Others', *San Francisco Sunday Chronicle: This World*, California, December 3, 1961, pp. 31-32, Omnibus Review.
Rosenthal, M.L., 'What Makes a Poet Interesting?' *New York Times Book Review*, New York, December 24, 1961, pp. 4, 14, Omnibus Review.
Delancey, Rose Mary, 'Poets' Views of Their World Differ Widely', *News Sentinel*, Fort Wayne, Indiana, February 10, 1962, p. 4A, Omnibus Review.
Johnson, Carol, 'Four Poets', *Sewanee Review*, 70:3, Sewanee, Tennessee, July-September, 1962, pp. 517-522, Omnibus Review.
Beum, Robert, 'Modern Miscellany', *Prairie Schooner*, 36:3, Lincoln, Nebraska, Autumn, 1962, pp. 279-281, Omnibus Review.
Simon, John, 'More Brass than Enduring', *Hudson Review*, 15:3, New York, Autumn, 1962, pp. [455]-468, Omnibus Review.
Morse, Samuel F., 'Poetry 1961: a Score or More', *Contemporary Literature*, 3:1, Madison,

Wisconsin, Winter, 1962, pp. 49-64, Omnibus Review.
Anonymous, 'Poetry', *Gazette*, Berkeley, California, July, 1963, p. 12, Omnibus Review.
Talbot, Norman, '... From America', *Poetry Australia*, 1:6, Sydney, October, 1965, p. 40, Omnibus Review.
McConathy, Dale, 'The Poet and the Jukebox', *Harper's Bazaar*, 100:3050, New York, January, 1966, p. 165, Omnibus Review.

Selected Poems by Thom Gunn and Ted Hughes (Faber and Faber, 1962)

Dale, Peter, Untitled, *Agenda*, 2:9-10, London, September-October, 1962, pp. 17-19.
Symons, Julian, 'Poems Paperback', *Spectator*, 209:7009, London, October 26, 1962, p. 650, Omnibus Review.

A Geography (Stone Wall Press, 1966)

Anonymous, 'Notes on Current Books', *Virginia Quarterly Review*, 42:4, Charlottesville, Virginia, Autumn, 1966, p. cxl, Omnibus Review.
Roselip, Raymond, 'Our Land and Sea & Hallelujah', *Poetry*, 111:3, Chicago, Illinois, December, 1967, pp. 189-195, Omnibus Review.
Bergonzi, Bernard, 'Nature, Mostly American', *Southern Review*, 6:1, Baton Rouge, Louisiana, January, 1970, pp. 205-215, Omnibus Review.

Positives (Faber and Faber, 1966)

Bergonzi, Bernard, 'More Revised Versions', *Guardian*, Manchester, November 25, 1966, p. 13, Omnibus Review.
Connolly, Cyril, 'Laureate of Anglo-Saxony', *Sunday Times*, London, November 27, 1966, p. 53, Omnibus Review.
Anonymous, 'A Poetic Look at Life', *Cambridge Evening News*, Cambridge, December 3, 1966, p. 7.
Anonymous, 'Poetry', *Sunday Times*, London, December 4, 1966, p. 30, Omnibus Review.
Anonymous, 'Photographer and Poet', *Western Morning News*, Plymouth, December 9, 1966, p. 13.
Carey, John, 'Unpolitical Auden', *New Statesman*, 72:1867, London, December 23, 1966, pp. 941-942, Omnibus Review.
Anonymous, 'Mr Betjeman and Other Poets', *Times*, London, December 29, 1966, p. 12, Omnibus Review.
Marsh, Peter, 'Poems for the Camera', *Observer*, London, January 1, 1967, p. 25, Omnibus Review.
Puffmore, Henry, 'Under Review', *Bookseller*, 3185, London, January 7, 1967, pp. 48-50, Omnibus Review.
Anonymous, 'Tepid', *Times Literary Supplement*, 3386, London, January 19, 1967, p. 48.
Graham, Martin, 'New Poetry', *Listener*, 77:1974, London, January 26, 1967, pp. 140-141, Omnibus Review.
Cox, C.B., 'Scots and English', *Spectator*, 218:7234, London, February 17, 1967, p. 200, Omnibus Review.
Robson, Jeremy, 'Poetry in Brief', *Tribune*, London, February 17th, 1967, p. 14, Omnibus Review.
Kippax, H.B., Untitled, *The Sydney Morning Herald*, Sydney, March 11, 1967, p. 17.
Sealy, Douglas, 'New Poets', *Irish Times*, Dublin, March 18, 1967, p. 8, Omnibus Review.
Ross, Alan, Untitled, *London Magazine*, 6:12, March, 1967, pp. 113-114.

Evans, Barbara Lloyd, 'Poetry', *Birmingham Post*, Birmingham, April 1, 1967, p. 11, Omnibus Review.
Wilmer, Clive, 'Clive Wilmer on Thom Gunn', *Granta*, 73:1247, Cambridge, April 22, 1967, pp. 20-21.
Kelly, Henry, Untitled, *Dublin Magazine*, 6:1, Dublin, Spring, 1967, pp. 103-[104].
Sergeant, Howard, 'Individual Talent', *Poetry Review*, 58:1, London, Spring, 1967, pp. 48-50, Omnibus Review.
Sergeant, Howard, 'Poetry Review', *English*, 16:95, London, Summer, 1967, pp. [192]-195, Omnibus Review.
Dodsworth, Martin, 'Thom Gunn: Negatives and Positives', *the Review*, 18, London, April, 1968, pp. 46-61.

POSITIVES (University of Chicago Press, 1967)

Cushman, Jerome, Untitled, *Library Journal*, 92:9, New York, May 1, 1967, pp. 18-37.
Simpson, John, 'Human Tracks Across the Cityscape', *Christian Science Monitor*, Boston Massachusetts, May 4, 1967, p. B11.
Anonymous, Untitled, *New York Times Book Review*, New York, May 14, 1967, p. 20.
Pawlowski, Robert, 'Poetry', *Denver Quarterly*, 2:2, Denver, Colorado, Summer, 1967, pp. 172-173.
Lask, Thomas, 'Poetry As It Is and As It Might Be', *New York Times*, New York, December 20, 1967, p. 47, Omnibus Review.
Hunt, William, 'The Poem and the Photograph', *Poetry*, 111:6, Chicago, Illinois, March, 1968, pp. 405-407.
Anonymous, Untitled, *Virginia Quarterly Review*, 44:1, Charlottesville, Virginia, Winter, 1968, pp. xviii, xx.
Heyen, William, 'Fourteen Poets: a Chronicle', *Southern Review*, 6:2, Baton Rouge, Louisiana, April, 1970, pp. 539-550, Omnibus Review.

TOUCH (Faber and Faber, 1967)

Anonymous, 'Taking a Strong Line', *Times Literary Supplement*, 3423, London, October 5, 1967, p. 237, Omnibus Review.
May, Derwent, 'Impulse to See and to Sort Out', *Times*, London, October 5, 1967, p. 8, Omnibus Review.
Kavanagh, P.J., 'Out of Touch: New Verse', *Guardian*, London, October 6, 1967, p. 11, Omnibus Review.
Anonymous, 'Essentials of the Reticent', *Times Educational Supplement*, 27-34, London, October 13, 1967, p. 796.
Symons, Julian, 'Clean and Clear', *New Statesman*, 74:1909, London, October 13, 1967, p. 476, Omnibus Review.
Dodsworth, Martin, 'Taking Pleasure', *Listener*, 78:2012, London, October 19, 1967, pp. 506-507, Omnibus Review.
Robson, Jeremy, 'Five Poets', *Tribune*, London, October 20, 1967, p. 11, Omnibus Review.
Press, John, 'Zero and Nightmare', *Punch*, 253:6623, London, October 25, 1967, p. 639, Omnibus Review.
Williams, H.L., 'Marriage of Two Cultures', *Western Mail*, Cardiff, November 4, 1967, p. 8, Omnibus Review.
Hamilton, Ian, 'Dead Ends and Soft Centres', *Observer*, London, November 12, 1967, p. 28, Omnibus Review.
Oliver, Douglas, 'A Puritan Among Dabblers', *Cambridge Evening News*, Cambridge, No-

vember 21, 1967, Book Supplement, p. 4, Omnibus Review.

Owen, B. Evan, 'Troubles of Rootless Men', *Oxford Mail,* Oxford, November 23, 1967, p. 12, Omnibus Review.

Jebb, Julian, 'Poesy Triumphant', *Financial Times,* London, December 8, 1967, p. 28, Omnibus Review.

Seymour-Smith, Martin, 'Unafraid of Simplicity', *Weekend Scotsman,* Edinburgh, December 23, 1967, p. 4, Omnibus Review.

Jones, Brian, 'Poetry', *London Magazine,* 7:9, December, 1967, pp. 89-91, Omnibus Review.

Kell, Richard, 'Recent Poetry', *Critical Survey,* 3:3, London, Winter, 1967, pp. [178]-181, Omnibus Review.

Blachford, R.D., 'Poems: Ends in View', *Birmingham Post,* Birmingham, December 30, 1967, p. 11.

Eagleton, Terry, 'Recent Poetry', *Stand,* 9:3, Newcastle-upon-Tyne, 1968, pp. 62-73, Omnibus Review.

Gordon, Giles, 'Three Anecdotes, Four Slim Volumes', *Ambit,* 34, London, 1968, pp. 3536, Omnibus Review.

Nicholson, Norman, 'Poetry Roundup', *Church Times,* 151:5480, London, February 23, 1968, p. 6, Omnibus Review.

Blackburn, Thomas, 'The Poet as Craftsman', *Poetry Review,* 59, London, Spring, 1968, pp. 57-58, Omnibus Review.

Dale, Peter, 'Books Received', *Agenda,* 6:2, London, Spring, 1968, p. 95.

Sergeant, Howard, 'Poetry Review', *English,* 17:97, London, Spring, 1968, pp. 28-31, Omnibus Review.

Jennings, Elizabeth, 'Poetry, Formal and Formless', *Daily Telegraph,* London, March 7, 1968, p. 21, Omnibus Review.

Grant, Damien, 'Short Measure', *Tablet,* 221:6676, May 4, 1968, pp. 446-448, Omnibus Review.

Bolt, Sydney, 'Thom Gunn: Words in the Head', *Delta,* 43, Cambridge, June, 1968, pp. [12]-16.

Thorpe, Michael, 'Current Literature, 1967', *English Studies,* 49:3, Amsterdam, June, 1968, pp. 269-281, Omnibus Review.

Hayman, Ronald, 'Voznesensky, Elizabeth Bishop, Thom Gunn', *Encounter,* 31:1, London, July, 1968, pp. 69-72, Omnibus Review.

TOUCH (University of Chicago Press, 1968)

Skelton, Robin, 'Leaders and Others: Some New British Poetry', *Kenyon Review*, 122, 30:5, Gambier, Ohio, 1968, pp. 689-696, Omnibus Review.

Pawlowski, Robert, 'Seven Books of Verse', *Denver Quarterly,*100, 3:1, Colorado, Spring, 1968, pp. [100]-105, Omnibus Review.

Anonymous, 'Book Briefs', *Courier Post,* Weekend Magazine,Camden, New Jersey, March 23, 1968, p. 6.

Luddy, Thomes E., Unititled, *Library Journal,* 93:10, New York, May 15, 1968, p. 2009.

Jerome, Judson, 'Uncommitted Voices', *Saturday Review of Literature,* 51:22, New York, June 1, 1968, pp. 32-34, Omnibus Review.

Anonymous, Untitled, *Virginia Quarterly Review,* 44:3, Charlottesville, Virginia, Summer, 1968, p. cv.

Carruth, Hayden, 'Making it New', *Hudson Review,* 21:2, New York, Summer, 1968, pp. [399]-412, Omnibus Review.

Conarroe, Joel, 'Reviews', *Shenandoah,* 19:4, Lexington, Virginia, Summer, 1968, pp. [77]-

88, Omnibus Review.
Dunn, Millard, 'Through Poetry We "Find the World"', *Roanoke Times,* Roanoke, Virginia, September 8, 1968, p. C8, Omnibus Review.
David, Douglas M., 'Other New Books of Poetry', *National Observer,* 7:37, Silver Springs, Maryland, September 9, 1968, Omnibus Review.
Hine, Daryl, 'Critic of the Month, II: Several Makers: Poets and Translators', *Poetry,* 113:1, Chicago, Illinois, October, 1968, pp. 35-59, Omnibus Review.
Lieberman, Laurence, 'New Poetry in Review', *Yale Review,* 58:1, New Haven, Connecticut, October, 1968, pp. 137-149, Omnibus Review.
Grigsby, Gordon K., Untitled, *Per/Se,* 3:3, Stanford, California, Autumn, 1968, pp. 75-76.
Herzbrun, Philip, 'New Poetry: Is it "Trundling Along on a Plateau"?', *Washington Star,* Washington, February 16, 1969, p. D3, Omnibus Review.
Anonymous, Untitled, *Courier-Journal,* Louisville, Kentucky, March 2, 1969, p. F5.
Buchsbaum, Betty, Untitled, *Kliatt Paperback Book Guide,* 3:2, Newton, Massachusetts, April, 1969, unpaginated.
Korby, Kenneth F., 'Gunn's Poems and Walther's Letters', *Cresset,* 33:6, Valparaiso, Indiana, April, 1970, pp. 19-20, Omnibus Review.
Gildner, Gary, 'Gunn Ammons', *Northwest Review,* 10:2, Eugene, Oregon, Winter, 1970, pp. 129-131, Omnibus Review.
McMichael, James, 'Borges and Strand, Weak Henry, Philip Levine', *Southern Review,* 8:1, Baton Rouge, Louisiana, January 1972, pp. 213-224, Omnibus Review.
Martinez, G., *Hispania,* 1996, p. 1097.

THE FAIR IN THE WOODS (Sycamore Press, 1969)

Anonymous, 'Smooth Songs and Irish Echoes', *Times Literary Supplement,* 3504, London, April 24, 1969, p. 437, Omnibus Review.

POEMS 1950-1966 (Faber and Faber, 1969)

Symons, Julian, 'New Poetry', *Punch,* 256:6709, London, April 9, 1969, p. 547, Omnibus Review.
Chuilleanain, Eileen Ni, Untitled, *Dublin Magazine,* 8:3, Dublin, Spring, 1970, pp. 111-113, Omnibus Review.

MOLY (Faber and Faber, 1971)

Brownjohn, Alan, 'Gunn and Son', *New Statesman,* 81:2087, London, March 19, 1971, pp. 393-395, Omnibus Review.
Fuller, John, 'Acid-Head Allegories', *Listener,* 85:2191, London, March 25, 1971, pp. 381-382, Omnibus Review.
Porter, Peter, 'Change and Embroidery', *Guardian,* London, March 25, 1971, p. 8, Omnibus Review.
Wood, Michael, 'The Herb of Odysseus', *Times,* London, March 29, 1971, p. 9.
Marsh, Jan, 'Mystical Line in Poetry', *Tribune,* London, April 2, 1971, p. 11.
Hamilton, Ian, 'Soul Expanding Potions', *Observer,* London, April 4, 1971, p. 36, Omnibus Review.
Bosley, Keith, 'Metamorphoses: Recent British Poetry', BBC External Services and General Features Programmes, London, April 5, 1971, Transcript.
Anonymous, 'Separate But the Same', *Times Literary Supplement,* 3607, London, April 16, 1971, p. 439, Omnibus Review.

Seymour-Smith, Martin, 'Recent Poetry', *Weekend Scotsman*, Edinburgh, April 17, 1971, p. 3, Omnibus Review.
Andrews, Lyman, 'Lines of Violence', *Sunday Times*, London, April 25, 1971, p. 33, Omnibus Review.
Wilmer, Clive, 'Clive Wilmer on New Poetry', *Spectator*, 226:7457, London, May 29, 1971, pp. 742-744, Omnibus Review.
Peel, Marie, 'Thom Gunn's Cool Fantasy', *Books and Bookmen*, 188, 16:8, London, May, 1971, pp. 22-23.
Cox, C.B., 'Editorial', *Critical Quarterly*, 13:1, London, Spring, 1971, pp. [3]-4.
Fried, Michael, 'Approximations', *the Review*, 25, London, Spring, 1971, pp. [59]-60.
Green, Martin, 'Of Pigs and People', *Sunday Telegraph*, London, June 6, 1971, p. 10, Omnibus Review.
Rennie, Neil, 'Mystic Wisdom', *London Magazine*, 11:2, London, June-July, 1971, pp. 129-132, Omnibus Review.
Jebb, Julian, 'Darkness and the Light', *Financial Times*, London, August 5, 1971, Omnibus Review.
Dunn, Douglas, 'Damaged Instruments', *Encounter*, 37:2, London, August, 1971, pp. 68-74, Omnibus Review.
Lane, Travis M., Untitled, *Fiddlehead*, 90, Fredericton, NB, Canada, Summer, 1971, pp. 119-125, Omnibus Review.
Toulson, Shirley, 'Review', *Poetry Review*, 62:2, London, Summer, 1971, pp. 208, 210, 212-214, Omnibus Review.
Lindsay, Noel, 'Two Modern Poets Provide Marked Contrast in Styles', *Daily Journal*, Caracas, September 16, 1971, p. 19.
Burgess, Tony, Untitled, *School Librarian*, 19:3, London, September, 1971, p. 244, Omnibus Review.
Meredith, Ralph, Untitled, *Outposts*, 90, Surrey, Autumn, 1971, pp. 26-29, Omnibus Review.
Sergeant, Howard, 'Poetry Review', *English*, 20:108, London, Autumn, 1971, pp. [1-6]-109, Omnibus Review.
Wise, Nan, Untitled, *Speech and Drama*, 20:3, Wiltshire, Autumn, 1971, pp. 29-30.
Cluysenaar, Anne, 'New Poetry', *Stand*, 12:4, Newcastle-upon-Tyne, 1971, pp. 68-75, Omnibus Review.
Davie, Donald, 'The Rhetoric of Emotion', *Times Literary Supplement*, 3682, September 29, 1972, pp. 1141-1143.
Lehmann, L., 'Th. Poezie Routine', *Litterair Passpoort*, 27:261, Amsterdam, August-September, 1972, Omnibus Review, (in Dutch).
Kell, Richard, 'Recent Poetry', *Critical Survey*, 5:4, London, Summer, 1972, pp. 268-270, Omnibus Review.

MOLY AND MY SAD CAPTAINS (Farrar, Straus and Giroux, 1973)

Anonymous, Untitled, *Kirkus Review*, 4:4, New York, February 15, 1975, p. 229.
Luddy, Thomas E., Untitled, *Literary Journal*, 98:7, New York, April 1, 1973, p. 1173.
Howard, Richard, 'Ecstasies and Decorum', *Parnassus*, 2:2, New York, Spring-Summer, 1974, pp. 213-220, Omnibus Review.
O'Hara, T., Untitled, *Best Sellers*, 33:11, Washington, September 1, 1973, p. 251, Omnibus Review.
Perloff, Marjorie G., 'Roots and Blossoms', *Washington Post Book World*, Washington, September 16, 1973, pp. 6-7, Omnibus Review.
Spender, Stephen, 'Can Poetry be Reviewed?', *New York Review of Books*, 20:14, New

York, September 20, 1973, pp. 8, 10-14, Omnibus Review.
Anonymous, Untitled, *Choice,* 10:7, Middletown, Connecticut, September, 1973, p. 976.
Maynard, Temple, Untitled, *West Coast Review,* 8:3, Burnaby, B.C., Canada, January, 1974, pp. 57-58.
Allen, Dick, 'The Gift to be Simple', *Poetry,* 124:2, Chicago, Illinois, May, 1974, pp. 103-116, Omnibus Review.
Oliver, Raymond, 'Thom Gunn's Cornucopia', *Southern Review,* 11:3, Baton Rouge, Louisiana, July, 1975, pp. 708-711, Omnibus Review.

TO THE AIR (David R. Godine, 1974)

Grumbach, Doris, 'Fine Print', *New Republic,* 3091, 170:14, Washington, April 6, 1974, pp. 32-33, Omnibus Review.
Swann, Brian, Untitled, *Library Journal,* 99:11, New York, June 1, 1974, p. 1551, Omnibus Review.
Bromwich, David, Untitled, *New York Times Book Review,* New York, June 16, 1974, pp. 6-7, Omnibus Review.
Anonymous, Untitled, *Choice,* 11:5-6, Middletown, Connecticut, July-August, 1974, pp. 754-755, Omnibus Review.
Anonymous, 'Reserves of Energy', *Times Literary Supplement,* 3782, London, August 30, 1974, p. 932, Omnibus Review.
Oliver, Raymond, 'Thom Gunn's Cornucopia', *Southern Review,* 11:3, Baton Rouge, Louisiana, July, 1975, 708-711, Omnibus Review.
Inez, Colette, 'Especially for Meter Readers', *Parnassus,* 3:2, New York, Spring-Summer, 1975, pp. 173-182, Omnibus Review.
Powell, Neil, 'Air and Variations', *PN Review,* 4:4, Manchester, September, 1977, pp. 59-61.
Shaw, Robert B., 'Godine's Chapbooks', *Poetry,* 126:6, Chicago, Illinois, September, 1975, pp. 352-357, Omnibus Review.

JACK STRAW'S CASTLE (Frank Hallman, 1975)

Lee, Lance, 'Roots of Violence', *Chicago Review,* 30:4, Illinois, Spring, 1979, pp. 108-116, Omnibus Review.

JACK STRAW'S CASTLE (Faber and Faber, 1976)

Anonymous, 'Poetry Book Society Choice', *Bookseller,* 3691, London, September 18, 1976, pp. 1845-1846.
French, Philip, et al., 'Critics' Forum', BBC Radio 3 Programme, London, September 18, 1976, Transcript.
Bayley, John, 'Castles and Communes', *Times Literary Supplement,* 3889, London, September 24, 1976, p. 1194.
Brownjohn, Alan, 'Carnal Knowledge', *New Statesman,* 92:2375, London, September 24, 1976, pp. 417-418.
Cox, C.B., 'Wanted: Young Poets', *Sunday Telegraph,* London, October 10, 1976, p. 17, Omnibus Review.
Adams, Steve, 'Thom Gunn', *Gay Week,* London, October 14, 1976, p. 15.
C., B., 'Sensual Art', *Darts,* 406, Sheffield University, Yorkshire, October 15, 1976, p. 11.
Porter, Peter, 'Gunn Metal', *Observer,* London, October 17, 1976, p. 39.
Booth, Martin, 'Established Poets, New Approaches', *Tribune,* London, October 22, 1976, p.

8, Omnibus Review.

Dodsworth, Martin, 'Seductive Graces', *Guardian,* London and Manchester, October 28, 1976, p. 15, Omnibus Review.

Nye, Robert, 'Poetry', *Times,* London, October 28, 1976, p. 20, Omnibus Review.

Mitchell, Julian, 'Beneath the Poses', *Gay News,* 105, London, October 21-November 3, 1976, p. 23.

Sharratt, Bernard, 'Visions of the Moment', *Tablet,* 230:7112, London, October 30, 1976, pp. 1047-1048, Omnibus Review.

Symons, Julian, 'Beautiful and Damned: the Tyranny of Cities', *Sunday Times,* London, November 14, 1976, p. 41, Omnibus Review.

Blachford, R.D., 'Trying to Break Out', *Birmingham Post,* Birmingham, November 19, 1976, Post Saturday Magazine, p. 2.

May, Derwent, 'Burdens', *Listener,* 96:2485, London, November 25, 1976, p. 686, Omnibus Review.

Falck, Colin, 'Uncertain Violence: Colin Falck on the Poetry of Thom Gunn', *New Review,* 3:32, London, November, 1976, pp. 37-41.

Melly, George, 'Books of the Year', *Observer,* London, December 12, 1976, p. 26, Omnibus Review.

Boland, Eavan, 'Yesterday's New Voice', *Irish Times,* Dublin, December 18, 1976, p. 8.

Seymour-Smith, Martin, 'Poetry Now', *Financial Times,* London, December 30, 1976, p. 8, Omnibus Review.

Toulson, S., Untitled, *British Book News,* London, December, 1976, p. 942.

Johnstone, Robert, Untitled, *Fortnight,* 140, Belfast, January 14, 1977, p. 10.

Raine, Craig, 'Bad Trip', *London Magazine,* 17:1, London, April-May, 1977, pp. 96-101.

Chambers, Douglas, 'Jack Straw's Castle', *Body Politic,* 34, Toronto, June, 1977, p. 16.

Maynard, Temple, 'Thom Gunn, *Jack Straw's Castle,* London, 1976', *West Coast Review,* 12:1, Burnaby, British Columbia, June, 1977, pp. 70-71.

Powell, Neil, 'Air and Variations', *PN Review,* 4:4, Manchester, September, 1977, pp. 59-61, Omnibus Review.

Swinden, Patrick, 'Thom Gunn's Castle', *Critical Quarterly,* 19:3, Manchester, Autumn, 1977, pp. 43-61.

Cleary, A.A., Untitled, *Thames Poetry,* 1:3, Middlesex, Winter, 1977, pp. 66-73.

Eagleton, Terry, 'New Poetry', *Stand,* 18:3, Newcastle-upon-Tyne, 1977, pp. 75-78, Omnibus Review.

Wilmer, Clive, 'Definition and Flow: a Personal Reading of Thom Gunn', *PN Review,* 5:3, Manchester, May, 1978, pp. 51-57.

JACK STRAW'S CASTLE (Farrar, Straus and Giroux, 1976)

Austin, Roger, 'Books', *San Francisco Sentinel, 3:21,* California, October 7, 1976, pp. 8, 11.

Taylor, Brian, 'Sensual Epiphanies', *Globe-Democrat,* St Louis, Missouri, January 1-2, 1977, p. 6D.

McKenzie, James, Untitled, *Library Journal,* 102:2, New York, January 15, 1977, p. 205.

Raborg, Frederick A., 'American Review Ceases Publication: Solotarof Goes Out with a "Bang"', *Bakersfield Californian,* Bakersfield, California, February 11, 1977, p. 33, Omnibus Review.

Anonymous, Untitled, *Choice,* 13:12, Middletown, Connecticut, February, 1977, p. 1596.

Rosenblum, Harriett S., 'Poetry's Problems', *Democrat and Chronicle,* Rochester, New York., March 13, 1977, p. 2G, Omnibus Review.

Cotter, James Finn, 'Poetry of Apocalypse', *America,* 3483, 136:13, New York, April 2, 1977, pp. 295-297, Omnibus Review.

Anonymous, Untitled, *Virginia Quarterly Review*, 53:2, Charlottesville, Virginia, Spring, 1977, pp. 56, 58.

Cassity, Turner, 'Palo Alto and the Pampa', *Parnassus*, 5:2, New York, Spring-Summer, 1977, pp. 243-255, Omnibus Review.

Scoble, W.I., Untitled, *Advocate*, 220, San Mateo, California, July 27, 1977, p. 40.

Blevins, Steven, 'Poetry', *Gay Community News*, 5:5, Boston, Massachusetts, July 30, 1977, Literary Supplement, p. 7, Omnibus Review.

Lesser, Wendy, 'Senses and Endings', *Berkeley Graduate*, Berkeley, California, October, 1977, p. 7.

T., M., Untitled, *Kliatt Young Adult Paperback Book Guide*, 12:3, Newton, Massachusetts, Spring, 1978, p. 16, Omnibus Review.

Schramm, D.G.H., Untitled, *Boston Gay Review*, 4-5, Boston, Massachusetts, Autumn, 1978, pp. 8-9.

Harrison, K., 'A Round of Poets', *Carleton Miscellany*, 17:2-3, Northfield, Minnesota, Spring, 1979, pp. 234-239, Omnibus Review.

The Missed Beat (Gruffyground Press, 1976)

Powell, Neil, 'Air and Variations', *PN Review*, 4:4, Manchester, September, 1977, pp. 59-61.

Games of Chance (Abattoir Editions, 1979)

Gioia, Dana, 'Poetry and the Fine Presses', *Hudson Review*, 35:3, New York, Autumn, 1982, pp. [483]-498, Omnibus Review.

Selected Poems 1950-1975 (Faber and Faber, 1979)

Barrs, Myra, 'Cool Fantasy of Violence', *Times Educational Supplement*, 3311, London, November 23, 1979, p. 21, Omnibus Review.

Barker, Paul, Untitled, *Times*, London, November 24, 1979, Times Books of the Year, p. 1, Omnibus Review.

Baker, Roger, 'Sorcery', *Gay News*, 180, London, November 29-December 12, 1979, p. 23.

Mortimer, Peter, 'Poet's Brilliant Comeback', *The Journal*, Newcastle-upon-Tyne, December 6, 1979, p. 6, Omnibus Review.

Turton, Glyn, 'Poetic Reputation', *Birmingham Post*, Birmingham, December 6, 1979, p. 6, Omnibus Review.

Ewart, Gavin, 'Cold Comfort', *Guardian*, Manchester and London, December 13, 1979, p. 10, Omnibus Review.

Bold, Alan, 'The Source of Human Existence', *Literary Review*, 6, Edinburgh, December 14, 1979, p. 11, Omnibus Review.

Duncan, Sally, 'Coming Down to Earth', *Oxford Times*, Oxford, January 11, 1980, p. 12, Omnibus Review.

Nye, Robert, 'Poetry', *Times*, London, January 17, 1980, p. 12, Omnibus Review.

Nicholson, Norman, 'Two Modern Poets', *Church Times*, London, January 25, 1980, p. 7, Omnibus Review.

Bayley, John, 'Facts and Makings', *London Review of Books with New York Review of Books*, 27:2, London, February 21, 1980, pp. 14-15, Omnibus Review.

Welch, Robert, 'Gunn of Authority', *Yorkshire Post*, Leeds, February 28, 1980, p. 9.

Stanford, Derek, 'Contemporary Verse', *Books and Bookmen*, 293, 25:5, London, February, 1980, pp. 49-51, Omnibus Review.

Toulson, Shirley, Untitled, *British Book News*, London, February, 1980, p. 117, Omnibus Review.
O'Driscoll, Dennis, 'Recent Poetry and Criticism', *Hibernia*, 45:10, Dublin, March 6, 1980, p. 17, Omnibus Review.
Mole, John, 'Two-Gun Thom', *Poetry Review*, 70:1-2, London, September, 1980, pp. 56-59.
Eagleton, Terry, 'Recent Poetry', *Stand*, 21:3, Newcastle-upon-Tyne, 1980, pp. 76-80, Omnibus Review.
Ewart, Gavin, 'Poetry in Britain, 1978-81', *British Book News*, London, June, 1982, pp. 336-340, Omnibus Review.

SELECTED POEMS 1950-1975 (Farrar, Straus and Giroux, 1981)

Anonymous, Untitled, *Publishers' Weekly*, 216:7, New York, August 13, 1979, p. 54.
Davie, Donald, Untitled, *New Republic*, 3379, 181:15, Washington, October 13, 1979, pp. 36-38, Omnibus Review.
B., E., Untitled, *Booklist*, 76:4, Chicago, Illinois, October 15, 1979, p. 326.
Thiemeyer, Jay, 'Two Poets are Musicians of the Written Word', *Atlanta Journal Constitution*, Atlanta, Georgia, October 21, 1979, p. E5, Omnibus Review.
Howes, Victor, 'Thom Gunn: Poetry on the Cliff's Edge', *Christian Science Monitor*, Boston, Massachusetts, October 26, 1979, p. 19.
McKenzie, James, Untitled, *Library Journal*, 104:19, New York, November 1, 1979, p. 2353.
Hall, Joan Joffee, 'An English Poet: Thom Gunn "sniffs" Genuine Qualities of America', *Houston Post-Sun*, Houston, Texas, November 4, 1979, p. 18AA.
Hall, Donald, 'The Music of What Happens', *Nation*, 229:15, New York, November 10, 1979, pp. 472-473, Omnibus Review.
Dirda, Michael, 'In Praise of Poetry', *Washington Post Book World*, 9:18, December 9, 1979, p. 11, Omnibus Review.
Drury, Maureen Sullivan, Untitled, *Best Sellers*, 39:9, Washington, December, 1979, p. 347.
Rosenthal, M.L., 'Intimate and Alien', *New York Times Book Review*, New York, January 20, 1980, pp. 20-21.
Anonymous, Untitled, *Choice*, 16:11, Middletown, Connecticut, January, 1980, p. 1443.
Scobie, W.I., Untitled, *Advocate*, 285, San Mateo, California, February 7, 1980, pp. 42-43.
Murphy, Richard, 'Fierce Game', *New York Review of Books*, 27:4, New York, March 20, 1980, pp. 28-30.
Cotter, James Finn, 'Poetry, Ego and Self', *Hudson Review*, 33:1, New York, Spring, 1980, [131]-145, Omnibus Review.
Smith, Dave, 'Trimmers, Rounders, and Myth: Some Recent Poetry from English-Speaking Cousins', *American Poetry Review*, 9:5, Philadelphia, Pennsylvania, September-October, 1980, pp. 30-33, Omnibus Review.
Woodcock, George, 'Above and Below the 49th Parallel', *Ontario Review*, 13, Princeton, New Jersey, Autumn-Winter, 1980-1981, pp. 101-112, Omnibus Review.
McClatchy, J.D., 'Summaries and Evidence', *Partisan Review*, 47:4, New York, 1980, pp. 639-644, Omnibus Review.
Rawley, James M., 'Good and Flashy', *National Review*, 33:10, New York, May 29, 1981, pp. 621-622, Omnibus Review.
Pritchard, William H., 'Weighing the Verse', *Poetry*, 138:2, Chicago, Illinois, May, 1981, pp. 107-116, Omnibus Review.
Hirsch, Edward, 'The Existential Imagination of Thom Gunn', *Southern Review*, 17:3, Baton Rouge, Louisiana, July, 1981, pp. 648-653.
Loo, Michael D., Untitled, *Kliatt Paperback Book Guide*, 15:6, Newton, Massachusetts,

Autumn, 1981, p. 27.
Lake, Paul, 'Old Adam in the New World Garden: Three English Poets', *Threepenny Review*, 4, 1:4, Berkeley, California, Winter, 1981, pp. 9-10, Omnibus Review.

T*ALBOT* R*OAD* (Helicon Press, 1981)

Shafarek, Susan, 'LJ's Small Press Roundup: Best Titles of 1982', *Library Journal,* 107:22, New York, December 15, 1982, pp. 2303-2308, Omnibus Review.

T*HE* P*ASSAGES OF* J*OY* (Faber and Faber, 1982)

Bold, Alan, 'Thom Gunn: the Tyranny of Topicality', *Scotsman*, Edinburgh, June 26, 1982, p. 5, Omnibus Review.
Porter, Peter, 'The Boys in Black Leather', *Observer*, London, June 27, 1982, p. 30, Omnibus Review.
Ewart, Gavin, 'Moving Verse', *Guardian,* Manchester, July 1, 1982, p. 8, Omnibus Review.
Reynolds, Gillian, et al, 'Critics' Forum', BBC Radio 3 Programme, London, July 3, 1982, Transcript.
Lehmann, John, 'Poet of Imagination', *Sunday Telegraph,* London, July 4, 1982, p. 14, Omnibus Review.
Scott, Peter, 'Quarantine Order', *Gay News*, 244, London, July 8-21, 1982, p. 51, Omnibus Review.
Anonymous, 'Double Target for Gunn Lovers', *Citizen*, Gloucester, July 9, 1982, p. 26, Omnibus Review.
Ricks, Christopher, 'Poet with a Head for Heights', *Sunday Times*, London, July 11, 1982, p. 40, Omnibus Review.
Davie, Donald, 'Looking Up', *London Review of Books,* 4:13, London, July 15-August 4, 1982, p. 19, Omnibus Review.
Hamilton, Ian, 'The Call of the Cool', *Times Literary Supplement*, 4138, London, July 23, 1982, p. 782, Omnibus Review.
Heath-Stubbs, John, 'Wearing Thin', *Tablet,* 236:7411, London, July 24, 1982, pp. 746-747, Omnibus Review.
O'Driscoll, Dennis, 'Thom Gunn – Poet in a Fix', *Sunday Tribune*, Dublin, August 1, 1982, p. 20, Omnibus Review.
Smith, Iain Crichton, 'Poetry with a Dry yet Radiant Passion', *Glasgow Herald*, Glasgow, August 9, 1982, p. 4, Omnibus Review.
Kemp, Peter, 'Gunn's Views', *Listener*, 108:2773, London, August 12, 1982, pp. 21-22, Omnibus Review.
Lucas, John, 'Pleading for the Authenticity of the Spirit', *New Statesman*, 104:2682, London, August 13, 1982, pp. 20-21, Omnibus Review.
Philip, Neil, 'Something Lost, Something Gained', *Times Educational Supplement,* 3450, London, August 13, 1982, p. 18, Omnibus Review.
Holmes, Richard, 'The Return of the Metaphysical Kid', *Times,* London, August 19, 1982, p. 9, Omnibus Review.
Duncan, Sally, 'Sensitivity Born of Understatement', *Oxford Times,* Oxford, September 3, 1982, p. 8, Omnibus Review.
Anonymous, Untitled, *Malahat Review*, 63, Victoria, B.C, October, 1982, p. 249.
Booth, Martin, 'Document of Life and Death', *Tribune*, London, November 5, 1982, p. 9, Omnibus Review.
Philip, Neil, Untitled, *British Book News*, London, November, 1982, p. 702.
Powell, Neil, 'A Part Solution', *PN Review*, 30, 9:4, Manchester, December, 1982, pp. 68-

69, Omnibus Review.
Mole, John, 'Recent Poetry', *Encounter,* 60:1, London, January, 1983, pp. 60-66, Omnibus Review.
Rhodes, Neil, 'The Poetry of Physique', *Poetry Review,* 72:4, London, January, 1983, pp. 53-55, Omnibus Review.
Williams, Hugo, 'Rough Types', *London Magazine,* 22:12, London, March, 1983, pp. 94-100, Omnibus Review.
Randall, Belle, 'Thom Gunn', *PN Review,* 33, 10:1, Manchester, Summer, 1983, pp. 26-29, Omnibus Review.
Eagleton, Terry, 'New Poetry', *Stand,* 24:3, Newcastle-upon-Tyne, 1983, pp. 77-80, Omnibus Review.
Henri, Adrian, Untitled, *Ambit,* 97, London, August, 1984, pp. 77-78.

THE PASSAGES OF JOY (Farrar, Straus and Giroux, 1982)

Anonymous, Untitled, *Publishers' Weekly,* 221:26, New York, June 25, 1982, p. 98.
Harris, Roger, 'Seamy Side', *Star-Ledger,* Newark, New Jersey, August 8, 1982, Section 4, p. 18.
Hennessy, Michael, Untitled, *Library Journal,* 107:16, New York, September 15, 1982, p. 1757.
Bartruff, James, 'Thom Gunn and the World of Castro Street', *Los Angeles Herald Examiner,* California, September 19, 1982, p. F5.
Anonymous, Untitled, *Booklist,* 79:3, Chicago, Illinois, October 1, 1982, p. 184.
Reynolds, Joseph, 'A Poet Changed by Modern Cities', *Worcester Telegram and Gazette,* Worcester, Massachusetts, October 3, 1982, p. 8E, Omnibus Review.
Caldwell, Mark, Untitled, *Village Voice,* 27:43, New York, October 26, 1982, p. 55, Omnibus Review.
Barnett, Allen, 'Clear English', *New York Native,* 51, 2:26, New York, November 22-December 5, 1982, pp. 36-37, Omnibus Review.
Abbott, Steve, Untitled, *Advocate,* 356, San Mateo, California, November 25, 1982, p. 30, Omnibus Review.
Shakarachi, Joe, 'Sounds and Visions', *Poetry Flash,* 117, Berkeley, California, December, 1982, [1]-2.
Brumer, Andy, 'Exploring an Exceptional Literary Mind', *San Francisco Chronicle,* California, January 2, 1983, Review Section, p. 1, Omnibus Review.
Kinzie, Mary, 'No Connection', *American Poetry Review,* 12:1, Philadelphia, PA, January-February, 1983, pp. 28-33, Omnibus Review.
Miller, Brown, 'The Latest Gunn Poems', *San Francisco Review of Books,* 7:5, California, January-February, 1983, pp. 19-20.
Marks, Jim, 'Thom Gunn: a Lyric Poet at the Peak of his Powers', *Washington Blade,* Washington, February 11, 1983, pp. 19-20, Omnibus Review.
Lattimore, Richard, 'Poetry Chronicle', *Hudson Review,* 36:1, New York, Spring, 1983, pp. [205]-216, Omnibus Review.
St John, David, 'Raised Voices in the Choir: a Review of 1982 Poetry Selections', *Antioch Review,* 41:2, Yellow Springs, Ohio, Spring, 1983, pp. [231]-244, Omnibus Review.
Cotter, James Finn, 'The Friendly Hand of Poetry', *America,* 149:3775, New York, August 20-27, 1983, pp. 92-94, Omnibus Review.
Bogan, Don, 'Energy and Control', *Threepenny Review,* 15, 4:3, Berkeley, California, Autumn, 1983, pp. 14-16, Omnibus Review.

The Occasions of Poetry (Faber and Faber, Farrar, Straus and Giroux, 1982)

Bold, Alan, 'Thom Gunn: the Tyranny of Topicality', *Scotsman*, Edinburgh, June 26, 1982, p. 5, Omnibus Review.
Porter, Peter, 'The Boys in Black Leather', *Observer*, London, June 27, 1982, p. 30, Omnibus Review.
Ewart, Gavin, 'Moving Verse', *Guardian*, Manchester, July 1, 1982, p. 8, Omnibus Review.
Reynolds, Gillian, et al, 'Critics' Forum', BBC Radio 3 Programme, London, July 3, 1982, Transcript.
Lehmann, John, 'Poet of Imagination', *Sunday Telegraph*, London, July 4, 1982, p. 14, Omnibus Review.
Scott, Peter, 'Quarantine Order', *Gay News*, 244, London, July 8-21, 1982, p. 51, Omnibus Review.
Anonymous, 'Double Target for Gunn Lovers', *Citizen*, Gloucester, July 9, 1982, p. 26, Omnibus Review.
Ricks, Christopher, 'Poet with a Head for Heights', *Sunday Times*, London, July 11, 1982, p. 40, Omnibus Review.
Blachford, R.D., 'Snapshots of a Self-Conscious Artist', *Birmingham Post*, Birmingham, July 12, 1982, p. 8.
Davie, Donald, 'Looking Up', *London Review of Books*, 4:13, London, July 15-August 4, 1982, p. 19, Omnibus Review.
Hamilton, Ian, 'The Call of the Cool', *Times Literary Supplement*, 4138, London, July 23, 1982, p. 782, Omnibus Review.
Heath-Stubbs, John, 'Wearing Thin', *Tablet*, 236:7411, London, July 24, 1982, pp. 746-747, Omnibus Review.
O'Driscoll, Dennis, 'Thom Gunn – Poet in a Fix', *Sunday Tribune*, Dublin, August 1, 1982, p. 20, Omnibus Review.
Kemp, Peter, 'Gunn's Views', *Listener*, 108:2773, London, August 12, 1982, pp. 21-22, Omnibus Review.
Philip, Neil, 'Something Lost, Something Gained', *Times Educational Supplement*, 3450, London, August 13, 1982, p. 18, Omnibus Review.
Holmes, Richard, 'The Return of the Metaphysical Kid', *Times*, London, August 19, 1982, p. 9, Omnibus Review.
Duncan, Sally, 'Sensitivity Born of Understatement', *Oxford Times*, Oxford, September 3, 1982, p. 8, Omnibus Review.
Anonymous, Untitled, *Booklist*, 79:3, Chicago, Illinois, October 1, 1982, p. 182-183.
Reynolds, Joseph, 'A Poet Changed by Modern Cities', *Worcester Telegram and Gazette*, Worcester, Massachusetts, October 3, 1982, p. 8E, Omnibus Review.
Hobsbaum, Philip, 'The True Professors', *Times Higher Educational Supplement*, 519, London, October 15, 1982, p. 22.
Caldwell, Mark, Untitled, *Village Voice*, 27:43, New York, October 26, 1982, p. 55, Omnibus Review.
Barnett, Allen, 'Clear English', *New York Native*, 51, 2:26, New York, November 22-December 5, 1982, pp. 36-37, Omnibus Review.
Abbott, Steve, Untitled, *Advocate*, 356, San Mateo, California, November 25, 1982, p. 30, Omnibus Review.
Ewart, Gavin, Untitled, *British Book News*, London, November, 1982, p. 701.
Powell, Neil, 'A Part Solution', *PN Review*, 30, 9:4, Manchester, December, 1982, pp. 68-69, Omnibus Review.
Brumer, Andy, 'Exploring an Exceptional Literary Mind', *San Francisco Chronicle*, California, January 2, 1983, Review Section, p. 1, Omnibus Review.

Mole, John, 'Recent Poetry', *Encounter*, 60:1, London, January, 1983, pp. 60-66, Omnibus Review.
Rhodes, Neil, 'The Poetry of Physique', *Poetry Review*, 72:4, London, January, 1983, pp. 53-55, Omnibus Review.
Soldofsky, Alan, 'From Occasion to Meaning', *San Francisco Review of Books*, 7:5, California, January-February, 1983, pp. 18-19.
Marks, Jim, 'Thom Gunn: a Lyric Poet at the Peak of his Powers', *Washington Blade*, Washington, February 11, 1983, pp. 19-20, Omnibus Review.
Williams, Hugo, 'Rough Types', *London Magazine*, 22:12, London, March, 1983, pp. 94-100, Omnibus Review.
St John, David, 'Raised Voices in the Choir: a Review of 1982 Poetry Selections', *Antioch Review*, 41:2, Yellow Springs, Ohio, Spring, 1983, pp. [231]-244, Omnibus Review.
Randall, Belle, 'Thom Gunn', *PN Review*, 33, 10:1, Manchester, Summer, 1983, pp. 26-29, Omnibus Review.
Bogan, Don, 'Energy and Control', *Threepenny Review*, 15, 4:3, Berkeley, California, Autumn, 1983, pp. 14-16, Omnibus Review.
Eagleton, Terry, 'New Poetry', *Stand*, 24:3, Newcastle-upon-Tyne, 1983, pp. 77-80, Omnibus Review.
Middleton, David, E., 'Green Branch and Living Root: Modern American Poetry and the Inheritable Past', *Michigan Quarterly Review*, 23:3, Ann Arbor, MI, Summer, 1984, pp. 435-445.
DiPiero, W.S., 'Poetry Defined and Self-Defined', *Sewanee Review*, 93:1, Sewanee, Tennessee, January-March, 1985, pp. [141]-149, Omnibus Review.
Marrin, J., *Modern Philology*, 95, 1997, p. 200.
Vermeule, B., *Modern Philology*, 96, 1998, p. 16.

THE OCCASIONS OF POETRY (expanded edition, North Point Press, 1985)

Gold, Herbert, 'The Good Long Read', *San Francisco Focus*, 33:1, California, January, 1986, pp. 69, 70, 98, Omnibus Review.
Gill, John, 'Musings', *New York Native*, 141,6:5, New York, December 30, 1985-January 5, 1986, p. 42.
Lesser, Wendy, 'Gunn Takes Kindly Tact in Criticism', *Tribune*, Oakland, California, January 22, 1986, pp. D1, D3.
Becker, Alida, 'New Paperbacks', *The Philadelphia Inquirer*, Philadelphia, Pennsylvania, March 23, 1986, p. 4.
Pratt, William, Untitled, *World Literature Today*, 60:3, Norman, Oklahoma, Summer, 1986, p. 473.
Tuma, K., *Contemporary Literature*, 34, Wisconsin, 1993, p. 266.

NIGHT SWEATS (Robert L. Barth, 1987)

Congdon, Kirby, 'A Thing of Beauty', *Contact II*, 53-55, New York, Summer-Autumn, 1989, p. 4.
Head, Gwen, *American Poetry Review*, 19:6, November December, 1990, p. 32.

UNDESIRABLES (Pig Press, 1988)

Hulse, Michael, 'Humane Actions', *Poetry Durham*, 19, Durham, Summer, 1988, pp. 35-38, Omnibus Review.
Wormald, Mark, 'A Place of Recuperation', *Times Literary Supplement*, 4461, London, Sep-

tember 30-October 6, 1988, p. 1079.
Powell, Neil, 'An Ocean Apart', *Poetry Review*, 78:3, London, Autumn, 1988, pp. 66-68, Omnibus Review.
McDuff, David, 'Poetry Chronicle', *Stand*, 30:2, Newcastle-upon-Tyne, Spring, 1989, Omnibus Review.

THE MAN WITH NIGHT SWEATS (Faber and Faber, 1992)

Walsh, John, 'Handsomely Mounted', *Bookseller*, 4493, London, January 31, 1992, p. 300, Omnibus Review.
Jenkins, Alan, 'In Time of Plague', *Independent on Sunday*, London, February 2, 1992, pp. 24-25.
Anonymous, 'Poetry Corner', *Western Morning News*, Plymouth, February 8, 1992, p. 12.
Calder, Angus, 'Tenderness with Rhyme and Reason', *Scotland on Sunday*, Edinburgh, February 9, 1992, p. 33.
Motion, Andrew, 'Posing Over, Pain Begins', *Observer*, London, February 9, 1992, p. 63.
Sinfield, Alan, 'Thom Gunn and the Largest Gathering of the Decade', *London Review of Books*, 14:3, London, February 13, 1992, pp. 16-17.
Mars-Jones, Adam, 'A Plague on Poetry', *Independent*, London, February 15, 1992, p. 29.
Anonymous, 'Testimony at the End of the Day', *The Economist*, 322:7747, London, February 22, 1992, p. 110.
Porter, Peter, 'Doing What Comes Naturally', *Sunday Telegraph*, London, February 23, 1992, p. xii, Omnibus Review.
Gillespie, Elgy, 'Poems of the Plague', *Guardian*, London, February 24, 1992, p. 33.
Sirr, Peter, 'Remembering the Lost Ones', *Irish Times*, Dublin, February 29, 1992, Weekend Supplement, p. 9.
O'Donoghue, Rory, 'Two Out of Three Ain't Bad', *City Limits*, 543, London, March 5-12, 1992, p. 22, Omnibus Review.
Horowitz, Michael, 'Battles for Humanity', *New Statesman/Society*, 5:192, London, March 6, 1992, pp. 46-48, Omnibus Review.
Brace, Keith, 'A Nation on the Right Lines', *Birmingham Post*, Birmingham, March 7, 1992, p. III, Omnibus Review.
Scammell, William, 'Not Quite Concentrating into Passion', *Spectator*, 268:8539, London, March 7, 1992, p. 32.
Spender, Stephen, 'Ode to the Body Beautiful', *Guardian Weekly*, London, March 8, 1992, p. 27.
Reading, Peter, 'Street Life', *Sunday Times*, London, March 8, 1992, p. 7, Omnibus Review.
Driver, Paul, 'In at the Death', *Financial Times*, London, March 9, 1992, p. xviii.
Gowrie, Grey, 'When Eden Fell to the Wiles of a Virus', *Weekend Telegraph*, London, March 28, 1992, p. 26, Omnibus Review.
Swarbrick, Andrew, 'Verses Aim to Mock the Pretensions of Poets', *Oxford Times*, Oxford, April 3, 1992, p. 15, Omnibus Review.
Nye, Robert, 'Grey Elegies Written from the Country's Graveyard', *Times Saturday Review*, London, April 18, 1992, p. 35.
Haughton, Hugh, 'An Unlimited Embrace', *Times Literary Supplement*, 4648, London, May 1, 1992, pp. 12-13.
Powell, Neil, 'Age of Anxiety', *Gay Times*, 164, London, May, 1992, p. 55, Omnibus Review.
Powell, Neil, 'The Dangerous Edge of Things: Two Views of Thom Gunn', *PN Review*, 85, 18:5, Manchester, May-June, 1992, pp. 60-61.
Wilmer, Clive, 'The Dangerous Edge of Things: Two Views of Thom Gunn', *PN Review*, 85,

18:5, Manchester, May-June, 1992, pp. 61-62.
Stocker, Stella, 'Celebration, Love and Lament', *Orbis,* 84, Nuneaton, Warwickshire, Spring, 1992, pp. 46-49, Omnibus Review.
Anonymous, 'A Guide to Summer Reading', *Independent on Sunday*, London, July 19, 1992, Sunday Review, pp. 32-33, Omnibus Review.
Paterson, Don, 'The Low Road', *Poetry Review*, 82:3, London, Autumn, 1992, pp. 56-57.
Jennings, Elizabeth, 'Books of the Year', *Daily Telegraph*, London, November 25, 1992, p. 4.
Glover, Michael, 'Books of the Year', *Financial Times*, London, November 28, 1992, p. xviii.
Morrison, Blake, 'Books of the Year: Poetry', *Independent on Sunday*, London, November 29, 1992, London, Sunday Review, p. 32, Omnibus Review.
Toibin, Colm, 'Books of the Year, 1992', *Irish Times,* Dublin, December 5, 1992, Weekend Section, p. 3, Omnibus Review.
Lemon, Denis, 'Books of the Year', *Gay Times,* 171, London, December, 1992, pp. 79-80, Omnibus Review.
Powell, Neil, 'Books of the Year', *Gay Times,* 171, London, December, 1992, p. 81, Omnibus Review.
Sinfield, Alan, 'Books of the Year', *Gay Times,* 171, London, December, 1992, p. 82, Omnibus Review.
Pybus, Rodney, 'Poetry Chronicle, I', *Stand,* 34:2, Spring, 1993, pp. 27-33, Omnibus Review.
John, Roland, 'Two Poets from the Sixties', *Agenda,* 31:2, London, Summer, 1993, 98-102.
Bayley, John, 'Death and the Captain', *Agenda,* 31:3, London, 1993, p. 93
Witemeyer, H., 'Thom Gunn's *The Man with Night Sweats'*, *Agenda,* 31:3, London, Summer, 1993, pp. 90-93.

THE MAN WITH NIGHT SWEATS (Farrar, Straus and Giroux, 1992)

Saylor, Steven, 'Thom Gunn in Love in the Time of AIDS', *San Francisco Review of Books,* 16:4, California, March 1992, pp. 14-16.
Coughnenor, Jim, 'Dealing with the Act of Love', *Bay Area Reporter,* San Francisco, California, May 21, 1992, p. 27.
Silberman, Steve, 'Elegies and Love Poems', *Poetry Flash,* 230, Berkeley, California, May, 1992, pp. [1], 4, 7.
Daniels, Peter, Untitled, *The James White Review,* 9:3, Minneapolis, Minnesota, Spring, 1992, p. 28.
Gilbert, Matthew, 'Furthering the Language of Sorrow', *The Boston Globe,* Boston, Massachusetts, June 1, 1992, p. 33.
Fries, Kenny, 'A Decade in the Making', *Lambda Book Report,* 3:5, Washington, July-August, 1992, pp. 16-17.
Triesman, Deborah, 'Rhyme out of Mind', *Newsday,* Melville, New York, August 16, 1992, Sunday Section, pp. 36, 38, Omnibus Review.
Smith, Joan, 'Writing AIDS Wrongs', *San Francisco Examiner,* California, August 26, 1992, pp. B1, B5.
Cole, Henri, 'Sketches of the Great Epidemic', *Nation,* 225:6, New York, August 31-September 7, 1992, pp. 221-223.
Dean, Tim, Untitled, *City Paper,* 16:36, Baltimore, Maryland, September 4-10, 1992, p. 17.
Anonymous, Untitled, *New Yorker,* 68:30, New York, September 14, 1992, p. 108.
Morrison, Richard, 'Books', *Art and Understanding,* 1:5, Albany, New York, September-October, 1992, pp. 28-29.

Pettingell, Phoebe, 'Poetry in Review', *Yale Review*, 80:4, New Haven, Connecticut, October, 1992, pp. 111-117, Omnibus Review.
Anonymous, Untitled, *Virginia Quarterly Review*, 68:4, Charlottesville, Virginia, Autumn, 1992, p. 136.
Randall, Belle, Untitled, *Common Knowledge*, 1:2, New York, Autumn, 1992, p. 132.
Logan, William, 'Angels, Voyeurs and Cooks', *New York Times Book Review*, New York, November 15, 1992, pp. 15-16, Omnibus Review.
Braintree, ?, and ? Burns [Pseudonyms], 'Book Chat', *Inches*, 8:8, November, 1992, p. 8, Omnibus Review.
Corn, Alfred, 'Looking Toward the Fin de Siècle', *Poetry*, 161:5, Chicago, Illinois, February, 1993, pp. 286-298, Omnibus Review.
Wilson, Joyce, Untitled, *Harvard Review*, 3, Cambridge, Massachusetts, March, 1993, pp. 184-185.
Wood, Michael, 'Outside the Shady Octopus Saloon', *New York Review of Books*, 41:10, New York, May 27, 1993, pp. 32-35, Omnibus Review.
Berger, C., *Raritan*, 13:2, 1993, pp. 141-155.
Bergman, D., *Raritan*, 13:2, 1993, pp. 141-155.
Dick, B.F., *World Literature Today*, 67:3, Norman, Oklahoma, 1993, p. 612.
Speirs, L., *English Studies*, 75:3, 1994, p. 274.
Bedient, Calvin, *Parnassus*, 20, New York, 1995, p. 95.
Dollimor, J., *Textual Practice*, 9, 1995, p. 27.
Landau, D., *American Literature*, 68, 1996, p. 193.
Crain, C., *American Literary History*, 9, 1997, p. 287.
Kaplan, D., *New Literary History*, 30, 1999, p. 221.

SHELF LIFE (University of Michigan Press, 1993, 1994)

Magowan, R., *American Book Review*, 16:6, 1995, p. 23.
Gwynn, R.S., *The Sewanee Review*, 104, Sewanee, Tennessee, 1996, p. 142.
Fenton, James, *New York Review of Books*, 44, New York, 1997, p. 12.
Stevenson, S., *College Literature*, 24, 1997, p. 240.
Golding, A., *Yale Review*, 39, New Haven, Connecticut, 1998, p. 180.

SHELF LIFE (Faber and Faber, 1994)

Lucas, J., *Poetry Review*, 84:4, London, 1994, pp. 15-16.
MacIntyre, T., *Irish University Review*, 24, 1994, p. 331.
Maxwell, Glyn, 'How Late They Start to Shine', *Times Literary Supplement*, 4746, London, March 18, 1994, pp. 10-11.
Toibin, Colm, 'Like Learning to Swim in Early Middle Age', *London Review of Books*, 17:8, London, April 20, 1995, p. 19.
Roberts, A.M., *Cambridge Quarterly*, 27, Cambridge, 1998, p. 129.
Lyon, J., *Essays in Criticism*, 49, Oxford, 1999, p. 1.

COLLECTED POEMS (Faber and Faber, 1993)

Bayley, John, *Agenda*, 31, London, 1993, p. 93.
Morgan, T., *Poetry Review*, 83, London, 1993, p. 62.
Maxwell, Glyn, 'How Late They Start to Shine', *Times Literary Supplement*, 4746, London, March 18, 1994, pp. 10-11.
Saunders, J., *Stand*, 35, Newcastle-upon-Tyne, 1994, p. 77.

Ward, G., *Cambridge Quarterly*, 24, Cambridge, 1995, p. 152.

COLLECTED POEMS (Farrar, Straus and Giroux, 1994)

Tillinghast, Richard, *New York Times Book Review*, New York, 1994, p. 10.
Gwynn, R.S., *Hudson Review*, 48, New York, 1995, p. 166.
Magowan, R., *American Book Review*, 16, 1995, p. 23.
McElroy, J., *World Literature Today*, 69, Norman, Oklahoma, 1995, p. 147.
Spurr, D., *Poetry*, 165, Chicago, Illinois, 1995, p. 289.
Klawitter, G., *Journal of Homosexuality*, 33, 1997, p. 33.

BOOKS EDITED BY TG

POETRY FROM CAMBRIDGE, 1951-1952 (Fortune Press, 1952)

Anonymous, Untitled, *Times Literary Supplement*, 2707, London, December 18, 1953, p. 814.

FIVE AMERICAN POETS (Faber and Faber, 1963)

Alvarez, A., 'Whatever Happened to Modern Verse', *Observer*, London, June 9, 1963, p. 27, Omnibus Review.
Furbank, P.N., 'New Poetry', *Listener*, 70:1791, London, July 25, 1963, p. 141, Omnibus Review.
Weatherhead, Benet, 'Coyotes Are Circling Around Our Truth', *Tablet*, 217:6428, London, August 3, 1963, p. 843.
Bayley, John, 'Book Reviews', *Agenda*, 3:1, London, August-September, 1963, Omnibus Review.
Anonymous, 'Moods Among Younger Poets', *Times Weekly Review*, London, September 5, 1963, p. 15, Omnibus Review.
Jennings, Elizabeth, 'New Verse: Form and Disturbance', *Daily Telegraph*, London, October 4, 1963, Omnibus Review.
Hall, Donald, 'Some American Poets', *the Review*, 9, Oxford, October, 1963, pp. [43]-52.
Anonymous, 'New World Poetry', *Times Literary Supplement*, 3218, London, November 1, 1963, p. 886.
Hunt, John Dixon, 'In American Waters', *Poetry Review*, 54:4, London, Autumn, 1963, pp. 259, 261, 262, Omnibus Review.
Stallworthy, Jon, Untitled, *Critical Quarterly*, 5:3, Manchester, Autumn, 1963, pp. 284-286.
Hollander, John, 'Poets and Places', *Encounter*, 22:1, London, January, 1964, pp. 67-69.

SELECTED POEMS OF FULKE GREVILLE (Faber and Faber, University of Chicago Press, 1968)

Holmes, Richard, 'One Glorious Moment', *Times*, London, October 12, 1968, p. 25.
Davie, Donald, 'Forgotten Poet', *Listener*, 80:2064, London, October 17, 1968, pp. 540-541.
Longley, Michael, Untitled, *Dublin Magazine*, 8:1-2, Dublin, Spring-Summer, 1969, pp. 86-88, Omnibus Review.
Anonymous, Untitled, *Antioch Review*, 29:2, Yellow Springs, Ohio, Summer, 1969, p. 266.
Anonymous, Untitled, *Virginia Quarterly Review*, 45:4, Charlottesville, Virginia, Autumn, 1969, p. cxxxiv.

Anonymous, Untitled, *Choice*, 7:4, Middletown, Connecticut, June, 1970, pp. 540, 542.
Rees, Joan, Untitled, *Modern Language Review*, 65:3, London, July, 1970, pp. 597-598.
Williamson, Colin, Untitled, *Review of English Studies*, 21:4, London, November, 1970, pp. 529-530.

FESTSCHRIFTS FOR TG

A Few Friends: Poems for Thom Gunn's Sixtieth Birthday, Stonyground Press, Walkerton, Ontario, 1989.

BIBLIOGRAPHIES

Hagstrom, Jack, W.C., and George Bixby, *Thom Gunn: a Bibliography, 1940-1978*, with an introductory essay by TG, Bertram Rota, London, 1979.
Hagstrom, Jack, W.C., and Joshua Odell, 'Emendations to *Thom Gunn: a Bibliography, 1940-1978* (Part I), *Bulletin of Bibliography*, 49:3, Westport, Connecticut, September, 1992, pp. 171-177.
Hagstrom, Jack, W.C., and Joshua Odell, 'Emendations to *Thom Gunn: a Bibliography, 1940-1978* (Part II), *Bulletin of Bibliography*, 49:4, Westport, Connecticut, December, 1992, pp. 263-268.
Hagstrom, Jack, W.C., and Joshua S. Odell, 'Emendations to *Thom Gunn: a Bibliography, 1940-1978* (Part III), *Bulletin of Bibliography*, 50:2, Westport, Connecticut, June, 1993, pp. 129-137.
Hagstrom, Jack, W.C., and Joshua S. Odell, 'Emendations to *Thom Gunn: a Bibliography, 1940-1978* (Part IV), *Bulletin of Bibliography*, 50:4, Westport, Connecticut, December, 1993, pp. 309-315.
Hagstrom, Jack, W.C., and Joshua Odell, 'Emendations to *Thom Gunn: a Bibliography, 1940-1978* (Part V), *Bulletin of Bibliography*, 51:1, Westport, Connecticut, March, 1994, pp. 75-106.

ARCHIVES WITH HOLDINGS OF TG'S CORRESPONDENCE

BBC Written Archives Centre, Reading, Berkshire.
Coleman Dowell Papers, 1950-1985, New York University Library, Special Collections, New York.
Donald Davie Papers, 1926-1995, Yale University Library, Beinecke Rare Books and MS Library, New Haven, Connecticut.
Howard Moss Papers, 1935-1987, New York Public Library, Rare Books and Manuscripts Collection, New York.
John Eugene Unterecker Papers, 1961-1987, Columbia University, Rare Book and Manuscript Library, New York.
Michael Mott Papers, 1950-1980, Northwester University Library, Evanston, Illinois.
Review of Contemporary Fiction/Dalkey Archive Press Records, 1980-1988, Stanford University, Special Collections, California.
University of California, Berkeley, Bancroft Library, California.
William Van O'Connor Papers, 1943-1967, Syracuse University Library, Special Collections.
Yvor Winters and Janet Lewis Papers, 1906-1982, Stanford University, Special Collections

The Gunn Archives

University of Maryland Libraries, Maryland.
Amherst College Library, Amherst, Massachusetts.
University of California, Berkeley, Bancroft Library, California.

The Critics

'[Thom Gunn] was widely considered the most interesting Cambridge undergraduate poet of his period, but his Fantasy selection does not perhaps represent him at his best. His poems are at once much more ambitious and complex in their scope, and less smoothly finished, than Mr Thwaite's or Mr Boyars's. He has, however, a special quality of his own, which might be described as a gift for imagining legend or for using narrative patterns, and not merely isolated images, symbolically ... Mr Gunn is obviously aiming at work on a larger moral scale than most of his contemporaries, and if we bear this ambitiousness in mind, even the occasionally rough and coarse texture of his writing is an encouraging symptom.'

Anonymous review of *Thom Gunn, TLS*, 1954

'Mr Gunn first attracted notice when three of his poems appeared in the anthology *Springtime* ... and although, as Mr Eliot once said in his lecture on Yeats, there are in any anthology "some poems which give you complete satisfaction and delight in themselves, such that you are hardly curious who wrote them ... there are others, not necessarily so perfect or complete, which make you irresistibly curious to know more of that poet through his other work." Mr Gunn's poems were of the latter kind; irritatingly clever and inbred, but bold and very well constructed. Unfortunately he has written nothing quite as good since then, and "A Mirror for Poets", "Helen's Rape", and "Carnal Knowledge", are the best in the book ...'

Anonymous review of *Fighting Terms, TLS*, 1954

'I can think of few contemporary poets ... who write with [his] kind of assurance and purpose.'

A. Alvarez, review of *The Sense of Movement, Observer*, 1957

'He states afresh and with great force questions which have troubled poets and thinkers in all ages. But he is aware of them as existing now, in his life, and he contributes something new to the old debate ... [H]is poetry is an achievement.'

Edwin Muir, review of *The Sense of Movement, New Statesman*, 1957

'Technically, Mr Gunn has greatly advanced since *Fighting Terms*. In the present book there is far less fumbling and the poems are better shaped. If there has been a loss at all, it is in the detail of his work; in the edgy, aggressive use of language and the impatient gestures that made his earlier poems so arresting. This book, however, establishes Mr Gunn as one of the few really interesting poets of his generation and promises greatly for the future.'

Anonymous review of *The Sense of Movement, TLS*, 1957

'He is clearly England's most important export since Auden.'

    Philip Booth, review of *The Sense of Movement, Christian Science Monitor,* 1959

'One of the most impressive features of Thom Gunn's work is its constant sense of change and renewal. Where more fashionable poets find a good line and stick to it, Gunn has developed ... *My Sad Captains* is another step forward, this time into a new clarity of theme and style ... [B]eautifully clear, firm language.'

    A. Alvarez, review of *My Sad Captains, Observer,* 1961

'This book makes it clear that Mr Gunn is one of the leading poets of his generation.'

    Bernard Bergonzi, review of *My Sad Captains, Manchester Guardian,* 1961

'It reinforces the conviction that Gunn is the best English poet of his generation.'

    Richard Mayne, review of *My Sad Captains,* BBC, *The Critics,* 1961

' ... *The Sense of Movement* raised such high hopes that one trembled to open his new book lest it should fail to fulfil them. The first poem ... removes all these fears, for in it Mr Gunn displays his old virtues – precision, assurance, sinewy vigour – and a new compassionate understanding of human needs ... wherever his impulse to explore may guide him we may confidently expect from him poems of an ever-increasing authority and power.'

    John Press, review of *My Sad Captains, Sunday Times,* 1961

'A peculiar and rather terrible starkness of attitude combines often in Mr Gunn's poems ... with a poise and lucidity of thought and language which it is often not absurd or even overstretched to describe as classical. In addition, the total narrative or ratiocinative shapes of poems are conceived like small dramas ... Mr John Mander recently described Mr Gunn as living in a state of existential pre-commitment. These lucid, anti-symbolic or non-symbolic poems certainly have the quality that the French call authenticity. The moral bleakness, the rejection of given values strengthen the occasional celebration of the heroic or knightly. Mr Gunn has a very notable talent.'

    Anonymous review of *My Sad Captains, TLS,* 1961

'Poetry is never easy to write, but it is certainly easier to write on Hughes's terms than it is on the terms Gunn, albeit clumsily, is attempting.'

    Peter Dale, review of *Selected Poems by Thom Gunn and Ted Hughes, Agenda,* 1962

'The early verse of an enormously gifted writer often has a peculiar tang and freshness that he never recaptures, even though he may later surpass his youthful achievements, and *Fighting Terms* contains a great deal of such verse, which is of interest also in that it foreshadows the themes of his subsequent poetry. This is one of the few volumes of postwar verse that all serious readers of poetry need to possess and to study.'

John Press, review of *Fighting Terms, Cambridge Review*, 1962

'*Positives* follows the stages of youth and age, from germ to gaffer, through the dodgem cars, warehouses, building-sites, chainstores of a modern city – London, as it happens ... The forms dancingly reciprocate: words authenticated by the camera, photographs loosed from rigidity by poems.'

John Carey, review of *Positives, New Statesman*, 1966

'The poems are a work of art in themselves, so are the photographs, and I warmly suggest *Positives* to lovers of both forms as worthy of prolonged meditation.'

Cyril Connolly, review of *Positives, Sunday Times*, 1966

'The photographs are superb, particularly the portraits. Pictures and verse interact with a rich expressiveness; this is a book to browse through with pleasure many, many times.'

C.B. Cox, review of *Positives, Spectator*, 1967

Gunn succeeds because of his fine certainty of tone and the sober dignity of his language. "Misanthropos", which occupies a third of the new book, is an imaginative achievement probably beyond the reach of any other living poet, and almost every poem in this collection shows the agility and subtlety of Gunn's mind and his ability to convey complicated ideas directly, forcefully and with wit.'

Julian Symons, review of *Touch, New Statesman*, 1967

'An oddly over-praised collection, this; Ander Gunn's drab metropolitan vision offers in its competence only a ringside view of the limitation of the medium, while Thom Gunn's verses, by fulfilling the obligation of captions, can do no more than lay bare the parodiable elements of his style. His mental and emotional reactions to his brother's work may here be continually evaluated in a way that poetry may not, and the combined result is more often supererogatory than sympathetic.'

Anonymous review of *Positives, TLS*, 1967

'Thom Gunn is an unsettled and unsettling poet: nervous, bleak, tense, edgy, committed to a brute masculine energy because, it would seem, he distrusts something altogether gentler, softer or more whimsical in himself. It is this tension which has given Mr Gunn his characteristic fine-drawn voice and made him a more interesting and problematical poet than almost any of his contemporaries ... It is a relief to find Mr Gunn no longer striking exaggerated poses, as he did in "Lines for a Book", "Elvis Presley", or, in its different way, "Crabs". The last poem in *Touch*, "Back to Life", seems to sum up, better than ever before, with a new openness and generosity of spirit, Mr Gunn's essentially grave, even melancholy, nature, and does it beautifully.'

Anonymous review of *Touch*, *TLS*, 1967

'In Thom Gunn's poem, it is not easy to work out what is going on.'

Anonymous review [reproduced entire] of *The Fair in the Woods*, *TLS*, 1969.

'Light in all its manifestations and with all its literal and metaphoric powers is the central theme of Thom Gunn's superb new collection of poems. The volume may be taken as a journey into light, ending with what is perhaps the finest poem he has yet written, "Sunlight" ...'

Julian Jebb, review of *Moly*, *The Financial Times*, 1971

'At both moral and aesthetic levels ... Gunn seems in this new volume to have broken beyond his former implication that the one alternative to a blank, existential alienation was a dangerously undermining empathy. Vigilant separateness and outgoing responsiveness can now be embraced within a single outline: and this is true at the technical, as well as the thematic, level ... *Moly* lacks the metaphysical drama of the earlier Gunn; but it represents a mature distillation of some of the major issues which he has pursued so ambitiously throughout his work.'

Anonymous review of *Moly*, *TLS*, 1971

'It is as though A.E. Housman were dealing with the subject matter of *Howl*, or Tennyson were on the side of the Lotus Eaters.'

Stephen Spender, review of *Moly and My Sad Captains*, *NYRB*, 1973

'The effort — and in such poems as "The Colour Machine", "The Fair in the Woods", "The Garden of the Gods", "The Messenger" and, chiefly, "At the Centre", the effort is not only made but mastered — is to get beyond definition, questions like "what place is this?", "what am I?", and into identification, into that surrender of the separating will which may then merely — merely! — acknowledge, acquiesce.'

Richard Howard, review of *Moly and My Sad Captains*, *Parnassus*, 1974

'It seems to me the case that quite a number of poets today, obviously distinguished, whose verses have made a merited mark, are not in the least concerned with making in us what Barfield called "this felt change of consciousness." In some cases — Thom Gunn's for me is one — not to do so seems deliberate policy. With him I have always felt myself grinding along, not alienated exactly, but clambering over and among the language to see what is going to happen next.

Thom Gunn's poetry has often seemed to me to be not quite "real", to be, as it were, counterfeiting poetry with a highly accomplished and covertly malignant skill, in order to draw forth and examine the relation of the consciousness of reader and poet – states peculiarly complex when both have before them something so unusual in the way of language as a poem, at once more expressive and more gratuitous than normal communication.'

John Bayley, review of Jack Straw's Castle, TLS, 1976

'The poet who has given us the lines of most near-to-Shakespearian power in twentieth century English or American verse could well be Thom Gunn ... If [he] could put away the vacant counter-cultural slovenliness of his Californian ethic (its best side is when it takes on a Gary Snyder-ish austerity and only 'the junk that goes with' being human drops away) he might be able to recover the faith which once tied him in with English poetry's finest traditions; he might at the same time be able to get himself clear of today's fashionably neo-primitive dissolution of the moral and social human being into his constituent compulsions and energies and become a late and much-needed recruit to the battered ranks of humanism. If he could do both these things, he might be able to give us more lines of memorable poetry than he has given us in most of his recent books – not least by channelling his toughness into the one place where at this point in our history and in his own he could most valuably channel it: into the disinterested hard energies of art.'

Colin Falck, review of Jack Straw's Castle, New Review, 1976

'*Jack Straw's Castle* seems to me an achievement in finding a voice. I had not expected to hear Gunn speak so directly, and yet with such a sense of vulnerability and trepidation ... [T]ime and again, especially in poems about physical love, he becomes tender in a profound way – that is, he now sees lovers not as hoplites in a never-ending war, nor as potential Tristans, but as individuals in the only abiding collective.'

Peter Porter, review of Jack Straw's Castle, Observer, 1976

'It has been claimed for one of my contemporaries that he has written "the lines of most near-to-Shakespearian in power in twentieth century English or American verse." This is an astonishing claim to make for anyone, and of its nature a claim that cannot be vindicated conclusively. Yet when I read the recent *Selected Poems* by this poet, my fellow-expatriate Thom Gunn, I found myself persuaded.'

Donald Davie, address to the Shakespeare Association of America, 1978,
reprinted in Older Masters, 1992

'Gunn's latest work, for all its newly-founded sensuous celebrations and delirious yieldings to blood-impulses, is merely the reverse side of the hard, thrusting, misanthropic egoism which motivated the formal leanness of his previous collections. The surf-riding rationalist hasn't changed his spots; it's merely that Californian sub-cultures offer an illusory escape from the pressing burdens of isolated selfhood.'

Terry Eagleton, review of *Jack Straw's Castle*, Stand, 1977

'So much recent verse is no more than that, just verse, words, all ears and mouth, that even a fine critic like John Bayley, in reviewing *Jack Straw's Castle*, seems to be on the lookout for nothing more. From what he says, he was so busy browsing through volumes and attending poetry readings, in the hope that something would make his ears prick up and his mouth drop open, that the real thing, genuine poems, the best of Gunn's volume, slid by without recognition. He is simply offended, even by the very funny, though unsettling "Yoko", which is the least of the best.'

Merle Brown, critical essay, *Missouri Review*, 1979, reprinted in
Double Lyric: Divisiveness and Communal Creativity in Recent English Poetry, 1980

'It is a pity that so many of the attractive, lighter, but wholly serious occasional poems such as the lovely "Last Days at Teddington" from *Jack Straw's Castle* are omitted, but it is a great relief to find a complete absence of that hippy silliness and self-regarding camp which has been allowed too much license in the recent volumes. There is a side of Gunn which seems to delight in letting through fragments of embarrassing triviality, sketches which could perhaps have been worked into larger, witty celebrations of sexual tenderness – poems to match, say, the concerns of David Hockney in paintings like "Peter Getting Out of Nick's Pool" or "The Sunbather" – but have been left undeveloped. All aspects of this weakness have been sensibly jettisoned. What remains, though, is a set of excellent Californian poems which are among the best he has ever done.'

John Mole, review of *Selected Poems, 1950-75*, Poetry Review, 1980

'It is fortunate that American readers now have a single volume of Thom Gunn's selected poems. With their undemonstrative virtuosity, their slightly corrupt openness, their atmosphere of unfathomable secrets and their intimacy, so like that of a reticent friend who has something crucial to confess, these poems strike a chord at once insinuatingly familiar and infinitely alien.'

M.L. Rosenthal, review of *Selected Poems, 1950-1975*, New York Times Book Review, 1980

'... I cannot help thinking that the impact of Gunn's work suggests not so much what is powerfully there but what is skilfully almost there, that lived and hymned descent into the Yeatsian ditch. Instead of strength, body, character, one feels exhaustion, timidity, the habitual chewing forward through the practise of poetry. It is not versifying that is wrong with Gunn, but the utter safety of an art which reduces everything to matter in the skilled hands of an artisan who doesn't really believe very much matters. And yet, in spite of it all, I think Gunn's *Selected Poems* still delivers valuable pleasures in its self-assured, competent footwork. There are beautiful feints and ghosts in "Misanthropos", "In the Tank", "Three", convincing angers in "Sparrow", and "The Cherry Tree" is a knockout. It should be noted, too, that Gunn has radically selected this book, including less than half of *Moly* and *My Sad Captains* and only one third of *Jack Straw's Castle*. Regrettably, to my taste, he has pruned poems characterized by what he calls "Particularities which furnish Hell ...", which would have made his impact more that "tale of wrestling with a stranger." Houseman [sic], I think, would have called Gunn's book a serious event, if too sober, too much "At the edge / of the understanding."'

> Dave Smith, review of *Selected Poems, 1950-1975*, *American Poetry Review*, 1980

'In Gunn's new book of poems, *The Passages of Joy* (yes, I'm afraid it is meant to be ambiguous) there is a good deal of "coming out" – coming out of men's rooms, gay bars and one night stands. Much of this, however, is done with the dizzy relish of one who has for years believed that he would never get to write about such things. The pose of relaxed candour fails to conceal the poet's essential awkwardness ... The most genuine poems in *The Passages of Joy* are in a group of nostalgic, flat and exact pieces about Gunn's dead friend, Tony White – in these, there is no hint of narcissism, nor is there any forcing of sentiment ...

In addition to the "autobiographical" fragments, *The Occasions of Poetry* carries a selection of Thom Gunn's literary criticism. For several years, he was a regular poetry reviewer both for the *London Magazine* and *Yale Review*, and sometimes he showed himself a sprightly hatchet-man. Unhappily, none of these pieces is reprinted here ... The book's effort is to present the author as reflective and benign. We see him as fond and skilful explicator of Hardy and Fulke Greville, and as awed apprentice to Robert Duncan and William Carlos Williams. There are also sturdy salutations for contemporaries like James Merrill and Gary Snyder and some avuncular encouragement for the not-so-well-knowns – Rod Taylor and Dick Davis. All in all, an agreeable, slight volume – not easy to connect with the poems ...'

> Ian Hamilton, review of *The Passages of Joy* and *The Occasions of Poetry*, *TLS*, 1982

'Any poet worth thinking twice about possesses *at least* an energetic mind; but it is the harnessing of this energy which makes for excellence. In Gunn's work an apparently unlimited energy of vision finds, variously, the natural boundaries which make expression – and clarity – possible.'

> Jay Parini, critical essay, *Massachusetts Review*, 1982

'Between them, these two intriguing if uneven books leave one marvelling at Gunn's literary-cultural pluralism. To write *on* both Jonson and Snyder is one thing, to write *like* both of them in a single volume quite another.'

> Neil Powell, review of *The Passages of Joy* and *The Occasions of Poetry*,
> *PN Review*, 1982

'Gunn's recent collection ... has little to recount beyond casual encounters and homosexual gossip, depressingly thin and banal for a poet who at one time promised to be the most intellectually resourceful of the younger English writers ... Gunn is now a considerably better critic than he is a poet, which is not in the least, one imagines, what he is trying for.'

> Terry Eagleton, review of *The Passages of Joy* and *The Occasions of Poetry*,
> *Stand*, 1983

'Gunn is a consummate craftsman, a poet for whom there is no significant difference between craft and inspiration ... [F]ew poets take such a conscientious stance in relation to their tradition, their own experience and their craft ...'

Belle Randall, review of *The Passages of Joy* and *The Occasions of Poetry*,
PN Review, 1983

'If Thom Gunn is underrated in England these days, he has only himself to thank. Auden's transgressions seem minor by comparison ... It's disconcerting to find a major poet writing at such low intensity, and I'm afraid it prompts the resurgence of an old suspicion: Gunn's immense talent is one which needs to flex itself against technical constraints, and his most successful poems are almost always ones with a clear sense of controlling (not necessarily metrical) form.'

Neil Powell, review of *Undesirables*, *Poetry Review*, 1988

'The photograph on the cover of Thom Gunn's new collection – his first since *The Passages of Joy* – makes it abundantly clear that the six intervening years have done little to shift his preoccupations. A youth lies basking on tenement steps, legs splayed toward the camera, a python easing itself towards his neck. But fears that *Undesirables* might prove a mere repetition of familiar themes, a rehearsal of provocative poses embarrassingly struck in the past, are dispatched as soon as entertained. This history of the 1980s, and the effect of AIDS on Gunn's adopted San Francisco, are crucial to this. The pamphlet's twelve poems are without exception distinguished by the unflinching directness of their author's response to lives lived "In Time of Plague" – itself the title of one of the pieces.'

Mark Wormald, review of *Undesirables*, *TLS*, 1988

'The "sniff of the real" is everywhere in evidence in *The Man with Night Sweats* – the sniff of an unglamorized California, of gay America, the messed-up urban America of Reagonomics. Yet so is Gunn's admiration for the tough vernacular traditions of sixteenth-century verse and his taste for such traditional lyricists as Fulke Greville and Ben Jonson. Unlike other would-be restorers of and returners to earlier poetic modes in the postwar years ... Gunn's choice of traditional lyric norms and forms has (almost) nothing in it of historical pastiche – no cultural nostalgia for the "antique drum". Gunn's appetite for couplets and stanzaic metres, epigrams and epitomes, the kind of repertoire available to a Ben Jonson, is everywhere at work in his new poems, but it has nothing arch or archaizing about it. It is never a sign of historical homesickness or cultural conservatism but an instrument for recording a new ethos. He writes of and from the modern climate, as if wholly at home here; these new poems have a claim to be some of the most authentic occasional poems of our time ...'

Hugh Haughton, review of *The Man with Night Sweats*, *TLS*, 1992

'*The Man with Night Sweats* is quite [Gunn's] most spectacularly uneven book yet. The problem lies in [his] failure to avoid the most obvious pitfalls of his chosen forms: much of the book is written in either the sort of chummy, democratic, slack free verse that is no more than a good writer's impersonation of lazy diction (a trick Gunn has been turning for so long he seems no longer aware he's doing it) or full-rhymed, clumping pentameter, most of it lousy enough to sit happily within the 'canon' of the New Formalists ... Happily, in the last part of the book, Gunn goes a long way to restoring most of his credibility with a fine series of elegies, dedicated to friends who have recently died of AIDS. Suddenly, all the little cogs and flywheels of the form start turning, as if he had only forgotten to turn the damn thing on; the form now fits the content perfectly, each successive, inevitable rhyme drawing the poem on to its inevitable conclusion, the rhythm slowing the delivery so that nothing important should be left out ... It seems that Gunn must write out of necessity or a sense of duty before he can do it well. It's some comfort to admirers of Gunn the man and of his early work that his poetic powers – for so long inexplicably on the wane – did not desert him when it most mattered.'

Don Paterson, review of *The Man with Night Sweats*, *Poetry Review*, 1992

'In [the final section of the book] Gunn restores poetry to a centrality it has often seemed close to losing, by dealing in the context of a specific human catastrophe with the great themes of life and death, coherently, intelligently, memorably. One could hardly ask for more.'

Neil Powell, review of *The Man with Night Sweats*, *PN Review*, 1992

'*The Man with Night Sweats* ... is a remarkable book, and not only for the way in which [Gunn] memorializes friends and acquaintances dead from AIDS: it makes for painful reading, certainly, but it is Gunn's great achievement to have written these elegies which memorably pay their respects and keep their eye on the subject, not the author ... and present a sensitive marriage of technical virtuosity and intense but scrupulous feeling in his favoured Renaissance forms.'

Rodney Pybus, review of *The Man with Night Sweats*, *Stand*, 1993

'In assessing the Collected Poetry of an established master, one is inevitably drawn to pluck from the treasure the handful of coins one finds personally interesting, though I had not intended to dwell exclusively on Gunn's use of form. That focus does, however, illustrate a unity of purpose that extends throughout the work, from the watchful early metrics through the syllabics, the reach and skill of the free verse and, in much of the latest work, a return to strong form that might be termed triumphant had it not been called into the service of matter so saddening. Always Gunn has written from that lost and loving centre between brain and body which thinks while it feels, and feels while it learns: that species of poetic consciousness, perhaps unique to him in contemporary verse, has never flinched from joy or mortality, and does not flinch from the lengthy raw detailing of hopeless sickness that has been so much of its work in recent times. The human frame, fighting its dirtiest war for years, has at last got its strongest poet in the lists.'

Glyn Maxwell, review of *Collected Poems*, *TLS*, 1994

'The level of achievement from *Moly* and certain of the *Poems from the 60s* on through *The Man with Night Sweats* is remarkable, not least of all for having been sustained for nearly thirty years ... It seems he becomes more adventuresome as he grows older and is not afraid to fall on his ass trying out something different. Sometimes the poems are so emotionally bald and direct that they are deeply disturbing. They say what they have to say very plainly. Or sometimes Gunn can sound just like Dryden or Rochester cruising South of the Slot.

But we might well look to the words of Fulke Greville, writing of his own work, to best characterize Gunn's poetry from *Moly* on: "For my own part I found my creeping genius more fixed upon the images of life, than the images of wit, and therefore chose not to write to them on whose foot the black ox had not already trod, as the proverb is, but to those only that are weather-beaten in the sea of this world, such as having lost the sight of their gardens and groves, study to sail on a right course among rocks and quicksands."'

August Kleinzahler, critical article, *Threepenny Review*,
reprinted in *Agenda*, 1999

'It is almost alarming to look back over the forty-five years of Gunn's creative work and recognize [its] internal coherence. One is examining a level below that of consciousness, in which craft and imagination conspire to facilitate the expression of unrecognized insight ... [H]ere is a poet of exceptional imaginative range.'

Clive Wilmer, critical essay, *Agenda*, 1999

'Gunn has always been a very bookish poet at the same time as he has been quite opposite. In his fascination with "the map of the city", the life of streets and bars, he has never denied his education or turned aside from the expressive resources it offers him. On the contrary, he has reached for them with (to use his vocabulary) greedy alertness. In the great value which he sets upon learning both academic and moral, he stands closer to the Renaissance Humanists than to the Modernists, and is magnificently at odds with the run of contemporary writing.'

Robert Wells, critical essay, *Agenda*, 1999